EASY WAYS TO LIFT YOUR MOOD

(overcoming low mood and managing depression)

Jennie Willett
&
Dr Peter Connell B.Sc. (Physiol.), M.B., B.S.

TSL Publications

First published in Great Britain in 2016
By TSL Publications, Rickmansworth

Copyright © 2016 Jennie Willett & Dr Peter Connell

ISBN / 978-1-911070-21-4

The aim of this book is to teach you how to overcome low mood and depression by empowering you to take control of your life in creating your own happiness and enjoyment from living.

Jennie Willett

As a lecturer in adult teacher education, specialising in the way people learn I also facilitated courses at a London college on personal development. Many of my students suffered from low mood, anxiety and depression prompting me to devise tasks to lift their mood. These tasks I have included in this book. My private practice covers personal development, stress management and cognitive behaviour therapy.

Dr Peter Connell

As a general practitioner I was used to dealing on a daily basis with patients suffering from depression, anxiety and a range of similar illnesses whether expressed or hidden. I found talking therapies often worked better than medication. This book incorporates many of those successful methods that eliminated the need for medication.

This book is dedicated to our students and patients,
past, present and future.
We wish them all a successful outcome from any help
and treatment they may require.

IMPORTANT

If your low mood has continued for longer than two weeks, first seek help from a medical professional before embarking on the exercises in this book. You can tell them what you intend to do and it will show your strength in wanting to recover. With many mental health issues, professional medical advice and diagnosis is important.

Winston Churchill suffered from recurrent bouts of low mood and he referred to them as the black dog. We shall do likewise.

CONTENTS

Part Two - The dent in your world: Dr Peter Connell

THE BOOK

This book is divided into two parts. The first part is a quick fix guide to improving your daily mood levels. With these exercises you will experience improved mood levels, however it takes 21 days to form a new habit so within 21 days you could have made changes that will benefit the rest of your life.

The second part, written by Dr Peter Connell, explains the physiological changes occurring in depression, and how simple exercises outlined in part one of this book can return these changes back to normality. This part of the book is of interest to doctors, therapists and to those who are intrigued with the scientific aspects of mental health.

This book is designed to provide the basis for your own personal mental health. Use a highlighter pen to highlight areas you wish to work on. Skip pages which are of no interest to you. Start anywhere you like; we recommend starting from the beginning, but the aim of this book is to put you in control of your mental health so you can if you wish start from anywhere.

We recommend the following:

- Pen.

- A4 lined pad to plot your progress and to write a daily journal.

- Highlighter pens.

- Small diary or notebook to record moments of happiness/improved mood.

You may do all of this electronically if you prefer but writing in itself is therapeutic.

DAILY JOURNAL

- Write in list (or prose form) all you are grateful for that day. (see further in the book for the reasons for this exercise)
- You may wish to do this first thing in the morning, last thing at night, or at both times.
- What exercises worked for you today.
- What you learnt about yourself.
- Daily or hourly schedules.
- A done list.

BEING IN CONTROL

The aim of this book is to put YOU in control of your moods. If you find what works for you from this book and you give yourself a programme, and it makes you feel even marginally better than you did, then you are beginning to gain control. You will realise that medication and outside events are not controlling you. To make life better for yourself, you will now know what techniques to use and you will start to regain control of your life.

Some of the benefits:

- You will gain confidence.
- Not fear relapses because you will have a programme.
- Spot early signs of depression or low mood and be able to take immediate action.
- Seek professional help/advice earlier.
- Know when to take time out to recover.
- Interrupt the downward spiral.
- Cope more efficiently with everyday life.
- Reduce fear and anxiety.

HAPPINESS

Before we commence the exercises, let us take a brief look at what happiness is and is not.

- You need to discover for yourself what makes you happy.

- It is often not what you think it is.

- Happiness comes from within; research has shown that only about 10% of what happens externally affects our happiness.

- We think external events affect our happiness more than it does. I remember a gentleman in a class I was teaching of men who had suffered strokes. Despite his illness this man had something from within that shone through his illness and influenced us all.

- We can't be happy all the time.

- Happiness is a feeling of contentment and peace of mind.

- Kipling said:

    o   'If you can meet with Triumph and Disaster
         And treat those two imposters just the same...'

Those words are written over the players' entrance at Wimbledon. Success and failure bring similar emotions which are both not real in everyday life. We cannot continually search for the feelings we get when we meet a new partner and fall in love, or pass exams, or win the lottery. Also the reverse is true, it may seem like bad things happen one after another but in time they do pass, if we look for the rainbow after the storm.

Normal highs and lows are part of our make-up; however continual low mood and depression needs to be addressed and that is the purpose of this book.

MAKE LIFE AS NICE AS YOU CAN FOR YOURSELF

Another aim of this book is to teach you to make life as nice as you can, whatever the circumstances. It isn't easy but once you learn what works for you then you will have confidence that you can make life as pleasant as is possible given your circumstances.

Unfortunately when you are feeling low others may offer advice or comments:

- What have you got to be depressed about?

- When life sends you lemons, make lemonade.

- Pull yourself together.

- Cheer up.

- There are people worse off than you.

- Or they just look uncomfortable because they can't handle it.

People who are rich, famous, good looking, successful need more permission to be unhappy because 'what have they got to be down about?' Well, low mood and depression doesn't work like that. Depression is an illness that can hit anyone regardless of their position in life. Fear, anxiety, low mood can hit at any time, to anyone.

Forgive their comments and lack of understanding and just hope that they never have to experience what you are going through. Lack of understanding by others:

- Can make you feel worse.

- Lead to feelings of inadequacy.

- Fuel anger and despair.

Accept the comments and don't even try to get others to understand. Learn to confide in people who are sympathetic.

THIS BOOK COVERS

Help for any type of mental health issue, regardless of diagnosis, including:

o   Depression

o   Stress

o   Bereavement

o   Redundancy

o   Unemployment

o   Difficult relationships

o   Being a victim of crime

o   Bullying

o   Chronic Fatigue Syndrome/ME

o   Burnout

o   Divorce/relationship break-up

o   Post-natal depression

o   Exam stress

o   Recovery from illness

o   Major life changes such as leaving school, moving house, starting university, retirement

o   **(You can probably add more to this list, whatever your situation that you feel is causing a low mood.)**

This book covers:

- A range from those suffering with depression and or chronic fatigue syndrome where they may not even be able to get out of bed at first, to those who on the surface seemingly are leading a 'normal' fulfilled life but beneath the surface are suffering a general feeling of sadness / low mood.

- Techniques which can be used in conjunction with medication and other therapies.

- A healthy way of life for everyone.

- Some activities which may need to be discussed first with a medical professional and we will highlight these.

MAIN AREAS TO ADDRESS BEFORE YOU BEGIN YOUR PROGRAMME

DIET, EXERCISE & SLEEP

For all of us these three areas are of vital importance and it is beneficial to look at these first.

Answer the following questions :

- Do you get on average 7 hours uninterrupted sleep per night? ….. YES/NO

- Do you exercise for at least 30 minutes three times per week? ….. YES/NO

- Do you mainly follow a healthy diet containing plenty of fresh fruit/vegetables with very little salt and refined sugar? ….. YES/NO

Well done if you have answered 'YES' to all three. You may wish to skip the next three pages, however, it could be useful to reinforce what you already know.

SLEEP

Sleep is vitally important. If you get more than 7 hours uninterrupted sleep, it may be too much and contributing to your depression and you need to check this with your GP.

For most of us 7 hours uninterrupted sleep per night is a luxury, especially if you are a parent with young children. What you can do is find ways to catch up on your sleep. Lack of sleep is one of the major causes of stress and other mental health issues.

Here are some tips for getting a better night's sleep:

- Make sure your bedroom is conducive to sleep, i.e. it is only used for sleeping and lovemaking and no other activities like a home office.

- It is neat, tidy and comfortable.

- Try to go to bed at the same time each night so that you get into a regular pattern.

- No technology in the bedroom: texting, checking and sending emails or Twitter/Facebook.

- Wind down before bed: finish using technology about an hour before you go to bed.

- Find out what makes you feel sleepy: it may be a warm bath, a hot drink, reading or listening to music.

- Ensure your curtains block out light. If they do not, you can purchase actual thick blackout curtains.

- Set your alarm so that you get up at the same time each morning.

- Lying in bed at the weekends is not always as good as it feels at the time and many books recommend getting up at the same time as in the week but that is your choice.

How you get a good night's sleep is individual to you; you may wish to research this further. Dr Peter has covered this in his part but you may also like to read *I want to sleep* by Harriet Griffey.

EXERCISE

It is proven that regular exercise will help lift your mood as well as being generally very healthy.

For those who are unable to exercise, there are armchair exercises which a health professional can help with.

For people suffering with depression they may have no energy to exercise so start with a small goal of just a walk to the end of the road, or a local shop; you can then gradually build up. Just do what you feel capable of at first.

Some exercise tips:

- 30 minutes walking at a good pace will release endorphins into the brain, which improve your mood levels.
- Walking in rural areas, parks, open spaces is more beneficial; however do make sure you walk where it is safe.
- Walking on a treadmill at the gym but this is not as much fun as the two examples given above.
- Swimming is an excellent form of exercise.
- Joining a gym and playing sports are healthy pursuits.
- If you find it really difficult to exercise start with a short five minute walk and build it up each day.
- On your way to work by train or bus, you could get off a stop before your destination.
- Take the stairs not the lift.
- Walk to school or college.
- Take a short walk at lunchtime if you are working.
- Join an exercise class.

- Join a ramblers association.
- Check what is available locally in terms of exercise classes.

Housework and gardening are therapeutic as well as light exercise.

Always check with a medical professional before commencing any form of exercise.

DIET

Whatever your weight, to begin with make small changes to your diet to incorporate the following:

- Fresh fruit and vegetables. (At least 5 portions a day but at this stage any improvement will be beneficial so start gently building up to 5, if you are not already there.)

- Leafy green vegetables, kale, watercress, cabbage, spinach.

- Brightly coloured fruit and vegetables.

- If you don't like eating vegetables then turn them into soup.

- Cut down on refined sugar, cakes, biscuits, chocolate, puddings, alcohol.

- Avoid processed food and ready made meals.

- Download a healthy eating app on your mobile and learn how to cook inexpensive nutritious meals with the occasional treat.

- Limit coffee, tea and as mentioned above alcohol. Instead drink more water and herbal drinks. Avoid fizzy drinks, squash and fruit juices.

- Eat more seeds and berries.

- Use food as medicine, find the foods that protect your immune system and start building a healthy body. Research what you need to eat and obtain a diet from your GP.

- Keep your weight under control; aim to be within your BMI. There are several apps which you can get on your mobile phone which will calculate your Body Mass Index.

- If you are overweight seek professional help.

- If you have an eating disorder, do seek professional help. There will be organisations within your area.

- Emotional eating is often part of low mood or depression; but if you set yourself small achievable goals to lose weight you will do more of what is successful and at the same time feel healthier.

SCHEDULE YOUR DAY

Whatever your circumstances but especially if you are suffering from depression or any other circumstance which gives you a low mood. Those of you who are working, in education or voluntary work will have some type of structure to your day but you may still need to structure the hours you are not working or studying. For those of you who are at home it is especially important. Do not make it too rigid so that it puts you under pressure. Have a loose plan of what you want to achieve during the day. This will slot in well when we discuss goal setting later in the book.

- When you are feeling below par you need to allow more time for tasks.

- Plan your day in advance; the night before is best but you could do it when you first wake.

- Shower/bathe. Dress to impress (yourself). For some the journey from the bed to the shower will be the most difficult of the day.

- Plan your meal times, especially with your healthy eating.

- Build in time for exercise.

- Have a 'to do' list but do not overburden yourself with stressful tasks.

YOUR FIRST STEP OF THE DAY

Is to take a shower or bath and for many suffering from depression this can be the hardest step of all, just getting out of bed.

- Make it the first task that you do as it takes a lot of energy but you will feel the immediate benefit.

- Grooming is all important. Dress to impress (yourself). It may sound crazy especially if you are going to be around the house all day and we do not mean in a tiara or a dinner jacket; just dress smartly whether it is a track suit or more formal. Clean and smart.

- You will feel and act positively if you feel good.

- To stay in pyjamas or scruffy clothes for most of the day will only drain positive energy.

- Good grooming is an essential factor in aiding recovery.

- Looking good on the outside ensures feeling good on the inside.

At times this will be the last thing you will feel like doing but try to make it the most important start to your day.

SO FAR, VERY GOOD

If you have followed most of the tasks given on the previous pages and arrived at this page you should already be feeling the benefit.

- Aim for small daily improvements.

- Each day rate your mood when you get up, during the day and at night. Give your mood a score out of ten. Aim to raise by at least one.

- When you wake in the morning your mood may be a 3. Check it again after following some of the tasks given in the book. This will tell you whether or not they are working for you.

- You could draw up a daily chart or use a diary and rate your mood throughout the day following each activity.

MOODSCOPE

This is a free account where you log in with your email address. You use cards which you flip to rate your mood. Then you are sent a breakdown of your score. It has excellent reviews on how it helps people monitor and regulate their everyday moods. You are given a score out of 100.

On their website it says that people who weigh themselves each day tend to lose more weight and people who wear a pedometer when walking tend to walk further. Moodscope works in a similar way. People who rate their moods each day tend to want to improve their moods and find ways of doing so.

- Log into Moodscope.com and see if it is something that you think you would benefit from.

- Be careful how you interpret the cards. It can be very easy to rate yourself the same every time for some of them. For example, the card that says 'proud': maybe you are someone who feels you have nothing to be proud about. Take time to think about it. Can you change the way you now feel and give yourself one extra point just for buying and starting the exercises in this book?

- For many people once they start using Moodscope regularly they are eager to keep their moods at an acceptable level and will do more of what gets them a better score.

MANAGING THOUGHTS

Recovering from depression begins with managing depressive thinking. This is difficult. You may need to seek professional help through CBT (cognitive behaviour therapy), mindfulness training or meditation.

You will hear people say, 'think positively.' If only it was that easy. Negative thinking can become a habit and it can be very hard to think positively if you have a lot of stressful events in your life, but you can learn to consider other possibilities for the way you are thinking.

If you are suffering from low mood and general feelings of sadness, you can try to do this on your own. Here are some tips:

- Learn to spot when you are thinking negatively.

- When do negative thoughts intrude?

    First thing in the morning?

    Last thing at night?

    During the night?

    When you are tired?

    When you are hungry?

Our thoughts drive our lives so if you are constantly thinking negatively it will have an impact on all areas of your life. It will affect your body language, which can say more about us than the actual words we speak.

Affirmations are instructions we give ourselves. These are used to build confidence. They usually begin with 'I am'; for example, 'I am calm, confident and in control'. In cases of low mood they are often used in reverse such as 'I am useless, I am no good.' These affirmations are giving instructions to the sub-conscious and the sub-conscious will believe what you tell it, so if you are constantly putting yourself down through negative affirmations, this will become your self-belief system.

DON'T DWELL, DISTRACT

Learn to distract yourself from your negative thinking. You need to find what works for you. The television does not distract. In fact when depressed, people are inclined to watch too much television and the quality of viewing will contribute to the person going into their depressive thoughts.

Here are some ideas that will distract your thinking:

- Read a book.
- Draw or paint a picture (it is not possible to think about anything else while you are concentrating on drawing or painting).
- Crosswords or word games.
- Sudoku.
- Play online word games, with friends. This is an effective way of distracting your thoughts. *Zynga Words with Friends.* You can download this on your phone.
- Write a story.
- Phone a friend.

LEARN TO CHALLENGE YOUR NEGATIVE THOUGHTS

Write down your constant negative thoughts and ask yourself the following questions.

Do I really need to think this way?

Do I have any evidence for thinking this way?

Am I worrying about something that might not happen?

Is there some aspect I am overlooking?

Is there another way I could look at this?

How would I like to think about this?

Is there any part of this problem I am discounting?

How would I advise a friend who was thinking this way?

For those of you who know the game bridge, during the bidding there are cards you can use to inform other players you are going to make a jump bid, these cards are STOP (in red) and ALERT (in blue). If you were to mentally use these cards every time you catch yourself thinking negatively it would help you to control negative thinking.

Not all negative thinking is bad. Negative thoughts can warn if things are not quite right and alert us to take action. The type of destructive negative thinking that is unhelpful are the thoughts which serve no purpose such as dwelling on the past or hopelessness about the future.

DEPRESSION IS FRIGHTENING

When depression hits for the first time it is a frightening experience. Here are some important points to highlight and remember:

- Seek medical advice if symptoms last for longer than two weeks.
- It is an illness like, for example, flu.
- It happens to millions of people.
- It is nothing to be ashamed of.
- It is not about having something to be depressed about, it just happens.
- It is not your fault.
- If you work at climbing out of the dark hole of depression you will emerge a stronger person.
- Your confidence will return.
- Many people, friends and family will not understand depression and may ask questions like 'What have you got to be depressed about?'
- If you had a broken arm, you would get more sympathy because you can see the injury.
- You will feel isolated and that is why it is important to seek help.
- Like the flu, it will pass.

SMALL STEPS

When depression or the black dog hits, the first reaction can be to get out of it as quickly as possible but unfortunately it is not as simple as that. Some attempts may prove successful, but in the main it will take its course. Set yourself up for small successes. Note these successful steps. You may wish to record them in your journal.

Low mood can sap energy so basic tasks and activities can appear like massive mountains to climb.

Until your energy levels return, take note of the following:

- Do only what is necessary.

- Do not over-schedule your day.

- Set yourself small achievable tasks.

- If you have a long 'to do' list spread it over several days.

- With your 'to do list' try setting a timer for five minutes for each task. We get the energy to do something once we have begun it.

- If your home is a mess, take the timer into each room and set it for two minutes. See how much you can do in two minutes and then move to the next room. As your energy returns you will be able to set the timer for longer.

- Create a 'done list' instead of a 'to do' list. You will then get a sense of achievement from tasks you have completed rather than getting despondent looking at a long list of tasks still waiting to be completed.

HOW PERFECTIONISM CAN FUEL THE BLACK DOG

There are varied reactions to perfectionism. Perfectionism has its roots in childhood where a child may feel that in order to be accepted they will need to be perfect; this behaviour continues into adulthood. Many recognise that perfectionism is unhealthy and therefore deny they are perfectionists. Others think perfectionism is a quality and are proud to be a perfectionist.

- Perfection is not achievable. Salvador Dali said never to fear being perfect because it is not possible.

- Excellence is achievable; that is being the best you can be without being perfect.

- Know when to say 'that's good enough.' Or, 'that is the best I can do and it will have to be good enough.'

- When life, relationships, health seem less than perfect then that can be fuel for the black dog.

- Many will avoid doing something if they cannot do it perfectly. Mistakes are our best teachers so if we never try how will we grow?

- Use the affirmation 'I am aiming for excellence.'

- Letting go of perfection will reduce stress and open up the road ahead for success.

- Successful people are not perfectionists as perfectionism holds people back from achieving their full potential.

- Do not strive for the unattainable.

- There is no such thing as the perfect life and it can cause low mood if you are striving for a perfect life.

ANXIETY & PANIC

Anxiety usually accompanies depression and low mood. It is common to have some degree of anxiety, however, if you think you are suffering from any of the following, seek professional help.

- Anxiety disorder, where everyday activities give a high degree of anxiety.

- Post Traumatic Stress Disorder following a traumatic event.

- Social Anxiety; fear of social situations.

- Phobias; severe where a change in behaviour is required to avoid situations.

- Agoraphobia (Greek for fear of the marketplace). Where there is a fear of leaving the home. Many experience panic attacks in super-markets which leads back to the root of the word.

- Fear of flying, travelling, the Underground.

- Fear of public speaking is the number one fear of all; your doctor might be able to give you something to calm your anxiety but far better to enrol on a public speaking course then you will learn to be in control rather than the medication being in control.

BROODING

Definition of brooding is where the same thoughts go round and round in your mind. This is very damaging to recovery.

Brooding can become a habit. We take a thought and then brood on it until it becomes out of control. It becomes obsessive and we are unable to think of anything else except that one negative thought. It may be a comment someone has made, or a fear about the future. We think about it so much it takes over our whole thought process.

Note the times of day that you do this, does it coincide with:

- Being on your own?
- Hunger?
- Boredom?
- Watching TV?
- Travelling?

Ways to distract general negative thinking have already been given in this book, however reading is not only an effective method of preventing brooding it has also been scientifically proven to aid recovery from depression and lift low mood. When first diagnosed with depression you may not have the powers of concentration to read. Find an easy to read book that keeps your interest. For example a crime novel. Start reading for just ten minutes each day. You may find that you cannot put it down and will want to read more.

ACCEPT, LET GO, MOVE ON

How you think influences everything that you do and it contributes to your mood levels.

- Let go of negative thinking about yourself and the world.

- Accept the past, let go and move on. (You may need professional help with this at first.)

- Move on, the past is another country, you cannot change it, you can only learn from it.

- Peace of mind is a goal to work towards. It is what everyone is seeking when they are recovering from depression.

- Acceptance is a huge part of recovery. Accept life with its balance of good and bad things.

- Good things do happen, it is just noticing when they do.

- Let go of unhelpful beliefs.

- Once you have let go of the past and accepted it, you have freed yourself for new horizons.

Exercise:

1. In your lined pad write down what you need to let go of.

2. Write some affirmations beginning with 'I accept........'

3. Choose some of these affirmations for moving on:

   I am letting go of all my negative thoughts about the past.

   I accept my life as it was and as it is now.

   I make the best of my life for myself and those around me.

   I forgive and forget.

   I am moving on with confidence.

You truly need to believe in the affirmations for them to be effective.

IT IS JUST A FEELING

When feeling low it is important to recognise that it is just a feeling and very often has no bearing on reality. As mentioned throughout this book, depression is an illness, like any other illness and general low mood brings with it feelings of sadness and hopelessness. If these feelings are dwelt upon for too long they can become reality. We all have different ways of looking at things depending on our life script.

- Someone who is newly divorced or separated and feels unloved, scared, lonely and a failure, whether they instigated the divorce or it was thrust upon them. Another person could see it as an opportunity to get their life back on track, visit new places and meet new people. It could be viewed as more of a failure to stay in a toxic relationship.

- Divorce is like a bereavement and needs time to heal.

- Losing a job is a form of bereavement and recovery time is needed but in time it could be viewed as an opportunity rather than a failure.

- We have a choice how we view what life throws at us.

- Feelings are not necessarily facts and they do pass.

Exercise

- A thought produces a feeling. Next time you are feeling something negative try to identify the thought that produced the feeling. By challenging the thought and changing it, you can change the feeling.

View change as opportunity. We all need to look for the opportunity in every situation. There is one if we learn to look for it.

ATTITUDE OF GRATITUDE

We can already hear some of you groaning!! All the self-help books say this, and the reason is that research has proved this does aid recovery. When feeling down one can tend to focus on all the negative aspects of life. It is like thinking has got stuck in a groove which goes round and round the mind continually. This exercise is designed to focus on positive aspects as well as negative. We are not asking you to change your thinking but to challenge your thoughts and see if there are other ways of looking at situations.

This is more effective if written daily in your journal. Or you can think of say five things and one for each finger on one hand and progress to all ten digits. Or you can do it electronically, voice recording or keying into your phone or computer.

Decide what time of the day is best for you:

- First thing on waking.

- Over breakfast.

- On the way to work.

- Last thing at night before going to sleep.

- Several times during the day.

At first it may be difficult to find anything you are grateful for. Here are some examples you could use to get you started:

I am grateful for:

- Being alive.
- A new day.
- Family.
- Friends.
- Shelter.
- Food.
- The weather.
- Neighbours.
- Radio/TV.
- School, college, university, work, charity work.

You could start with three things you are grateful for and then add to the list each day. Try to find new things to add so that your list is added to rather than just repeated each day. This should start you looking for things to be grateful for. It may be someone who smiled at you while you were out walking, or a compliment. When feeling down it can be easy to overlook the positive.

AVOID MAKING MAJOR DECISIONS WHEN DEPRESSED

This may not always be possible but it is best to defer major decisions until depression has lifted. The view of the world is different when depressed and may influence a decision which would later be regretted.

- Decisions made out of fear seldom work.

- Any decisions you need to make, write down all the pros and cons.

- If you are unsure, seek advice from someone you trust.

- People have been known to end relationships when in a low mood, thinking the other person is causing it, only to discover that it was a health issue and then later regretting their decision.

- Write down a list of decisions you know you need to make. Put the list in an envelope and review the list when you are feeling better.

- Try to avoid decisions going round and round in your mind, this will not aid your recovery or bring you to a workable decision. Everything looks much clearer when it is written down.

- Right now you could write a list of decisions which could enhance your life and either put away in an envelope for future reference, or discuss with your therapist.

- Avoid clearing your clutter when depressed; tidying your clutter is fine but be careful what you throw or give away; you may regret it when you feel better.

COGNITIVE BEHAVIOUR THERAPY
(C.B.T.)

CBT is a form of therapy which deals with the here and now. It examines thought processes in a logical manner to see if there are alternatives that the patient hasn't considered. This is a form of therapy which aims to put the patient in control. The aim of the therapist is to teach the patient to become their own therapist. It involves devising assessment tasks to monitor behaviour and reactions. For example someone who experiences panic when travelling on a tube train would start by experimenting with walking to the station on one day and the next day taking the train one stop until they can complete a whole journey. This is just one example.

People who suffer panic attacks are given assessment forms to complete which look for evidence for thinking the way they do. *Mind Over Mood* by Greenberger and Padesky is an excellent book with copies of several forms. People are given permission to copy the forms as long as it is for their own use which is generous of the authors.

- If you want to try CBT for yourself obtain a copy of the abovementioned book.

- Copy the forms and practise using them and the checklists that are given throughout the book.

- These forms can be used for depression, anxiety, PTSD, problem solving, stress management.

- Keep a supply of forms and a pen handy so they are ready for whenever you may need them.

- You may wish to start with a therapist who will teach you how to become your own therapist.

The whole aim of CBT is to put you in control.

LOOK FOR DAILY BONUSES

When you are in a deep black hole it is hard to see a way out.

- Look for small unexpected bonuses; life is full of them.
- List them in your journal.
- Expect them; head a page in your journal - Bonuses Today
- Here are some ideas:
  - o   An email from a friend.
  - o   An invite for coffee.
  - o   A sunny day.
  - o   Someone smiles at you.
  - o   You find a parking place.

The more bonuses you find each day and list, the more you will attract because you will be looking for them.

MANAGING CHANGE

Major life changes whether planned or enforced can effect depression and cause changes in mood. We are creatures of habit and we like what we know and are familiar with; even if we are not happy with the situation, at least we know it. That is why many stay in jobs or relationships that are no longer fulfilling because of fear of change and the unknown.

Many students when first attending university will suffer from depression. There are professional and voluntary agencies around universities to help.

- List changes that have been enforced upon you recently.

- List changes you have consciously made.

- Then make a list of what you learnt from both situations.

- What changes did you fear? How did they turn out? Were your fears founded?

Change is an integral part of life; aim to view change as exciting. Remember excitement is the flip side of fear. The feelings are similar.

A CHANGE IS AS GOOD AS A REST

Use this time while your mood is low to make one or two small changes to your routine. Create new pathways to your brain by effecting change. Sometimes we get stuck in a routine and with energy low you may not be able to achieve all the tasks you want but by introducing change you may get more energy.

Some ideas:

- Eat something different for breakfast.
- Eat breakfast in a different room or go out for breakfast.
- Eat a meal by a window overlooking the garden.
- Watch a TV programme that would not normally interest you.
- Wear something in a colour you would not usually wear.
- Shop in a different supermarket.
- Take a different route to work, college or the shops.
- Visit somewhere in your area you have never been before.
- Learn something new.
- Read a different newspaper from your usual choice.

Exercise:

Plan something small that you will do differently tomorrow and write it in your journal.

DO THE OPPOSITE OF WHAT YOUR DEPRESSION MAY BE TELLING YOU TO DO

Is your depression and lack of energy telling you to do some or most of the following:

- Stay in bed.

- Stay in bed later than normal.

- Sit in front of the TV watching whatever happens to be on.

- Eat non-healthy, sugar filled food.

- Drink more alcohol than is recommended.

- Stay indoors.

- Withdraw socially.

- Stay in pyjamas until past noon.

- Live amongst clutter.

- Spend too long visiting social media websites.

- Sitting staring into space for long periods.

Try to do the opposite. It will not be easy at first but you could set small achievable goals. For example:

- Set your alarm for a certain time and then get up.

- Bathe or shower immediately you get up while you have energy.

- Eat at least one healthy portion of food per day and then increase it to two, until you get to five portions or more per day.

- Go for a short five minute walk. Or just walk to the end of your road.

- Switch off the TV and listen to the radio for one hour.

- Limit time on social media sites.

- Send a text or email to a friend asking how they are.

These are only a few suggestions, you will be able to make a list of your own. Experiment with what works for you.

ANALYSIS PARALYSIS

It is common practice when suffering any form of anxiety, depression or low mood to over-think. Analysing thoughts because you hope that by analysis you can work your way out of the dark mood.

- This practice is seldom successful.

- Thinking goes round and round the mind giving a type of mental paralysis.

- It may be of benefit with an experienced therapist.

- CBT therapists deal mainly with the present so they are more likely to work on mindfulness and going forward.

- With some CBT books such as *Mind Over Mood* by Greenberger and Padesky there are forms at the back of the book with which you can professionally analyse your thoughts and this is recommended.

- Note when you feel this mental paralysing effect and use your 'STOP' card and then distract. Distraction will give far greater benefit (see page 35).

IDENTIFY THE OUTCOME YOU WANT

In your present situation what are you looking for? Tick what you are looking for and add some of your own. This needs to be in the present moment. It may change tomorrow. At this stage it is better not to look too far forward.

- More energy.

- Feel less tired.

- Feel happier.

- Less overwhelmed.

- Ability to enjoy life more.

- More motivated.

- More outgoing.

- More in control of emotions and feelings.

- More confident.

- More relaxed.

- Less anxious.

- Less fearful.

- Add some of your own:

(Note: these goals are not measurable and in time would need to be specific, but for now it will get you thinking in a positive manner.)

If you are working with a therapist, this will be useful information as it will enable them and you to set goals.

PREPARE YOURSELF FOR SUCCESS AND ACHIEVEMENT

Achievement is important when you are feeling in a low mood. Because your energy levels are below normal it can be difficult to start and complete tasks. When you complete a task it can raise your levels of adrenalin which then gives you energy to do more.

Exercise:

- Each day make a list of small tasks you could easily complete.

- At the end of the day, list all the tasks you achieved.

- Break larger tasks down into smaller manageable tasks which work towards achievement of the bigger task.

For example: you may have a pile of paperwork to sort. Set yourself a five minute task just to tidy and put it in a file ready for the next stage which could be to sort through it. This starts to put you in control of tasks rather than the other way round.

INCAPACITY

During some illness/incapacity, depression may accompany it. Even if you are bedridden you can exercise your mind:

- Music.

- Art.

- Radio plays.

- Reading.

- Studying.

- Crosswords.

- Number games.

- Writing. (Writing is an excellent form of therapy; it does not matter what you write; just write, no one else has to see it).

- Newspapers.

- Limited TV. Although readily accessible, it is not the best form of exercising the mind.

Experiment with what you can do to think outside of yourself and do more of what works for you.

LIMIT EXPOSURE TO THE NEWS

If your mood is low, constant exposure to negative aspects of the news can be depressing. You will want to know what is happening in the world so the news once a day is fine until you feel better.

With low mood, you will focus on the negative aspects of your life; one might be finance so if the news is disturbing about the general economic climate you may not be able objectively to view the news.

PUSHING THROUGH YOUR COMFORT ZONE

Social agoraphobia can be a by-product of depression (fear of social situations). When you know you are medically fit, it may be the time to start pushing through your agoraphobia and other phobias.

- It can creep up slowly without noticing.
- You start refusing invitations.
- Making excuses for not going out.
- Know when the time is right to start pushing through your comfort zone.
- We all need to push through our comfort zones; it is part of growing and we need to grow every day.
- Think about what you may need to do to start pushing through your own comfort zone.
- Make a list (not too long).
- Start taking small steps to regaining your confidence.

NURTURE OR NATURE?

Most of the students who attended my assertiveness and confidence classes regularly suffered low mood or forms of depression. What connected most of the students was a less than nurturing childhood.

- A child who has not received an equal balance of praise, discipline and love is more likely to suffer depression in adulthood.

- A child who has been overly criticised, bullied, abused or over-protected and not prepared for the wider world will often experience difficulties later in life.

- An adult who did not receive love as a child may experience relationship difficulties.

- Many throughout history had a difficult childhood but it did not hold them back in adult life; for example: Leonardo da Vinci, Isaac Newton.

- A difficult childhood can spur people on to make something of their lives and the lives of others.

- Some say an idyllic childhood is not always an advantage.

- Childhood moulds us but as adults we can change.

- You may need to discuss with a counsellor how you can move on from an unhappy childhood.

- Dwelling on the past will not change it; but learning from it can have a positive impact on the future.

THIS WILL PASS

Use this phrase when your mood is low; it is true. Anything which attacks your mental health is frightening but it can and will pass.

- With recurring depression/low mood it can feel as though you have had it forever, but it will pass.

- People who have felt suicidal know this to be true. That is why it is important to seek help immediately if you feel suicidal because the feeling will pass.

- Try writing each day in your journal 'this will pass'. You may not believe it at first but in time you will.

I WANT TO BE NORMAL

- Any form of depression isolates.

- It seems as if everyone else is 'out there enjoying life.'

- Although there is no such thing as being normal, you could try to identify for you what being normal is.

- Can you remember when you felt normal for you and you liked the way you felt?

- Maybe you can find a photograph of that time when you felt good and put it somewhere as a reminder of what you would like to return to.

- Each of us is unique. We are made up of our strengths and weaknesses.

- Our upbringing will have had a significant effect on our view of the world and our place in it.

- We may have taken the beliefs of those around us and they have become our beliefs.

- Is it time to challenge some of those beliefs?

OBSESSIVE WORRYING

- This can be a habit whether you are depressed or not.

- Nothing is resolved through obsessive worrying.

- Your worries overtake your everyday activities and drive you.

- You could try setting time aside for worrying.

- Set a time of day and allow yourself ten minutes to do all your worrying.

- You can write your worries down and when the time is up see if there is any action you can take. If not, shred the list.

- Each time a worry pops up in your mind, stop it because you know your worry time is tomorrow.

- 'I don't need to worry about that now, I can worry about that tomorrow.'

ANGER

Some forms of depression have been defined as anger which has been unexpressed and gone inwardly. Having roots in childhood, anger can surface in adult life when needs are not met. Anger not appropriately expressed can turn inwards.

- Anger is an individual emotion and it is difficult to give a generic coping mechanism, however it is unhealthy for it to go unexpressed.

- It can be frightening when one is consumed by overwhelming feelings of anger.

- You could try keeping an anger diary to see if there is a pattern.

- If you are angry about something that happened in the past and cannot move on, try writing a letter but under no circumstances send it. Write it and shred it.

- You may prefer to do the above exercise in the presence of a therapist.

- Not all anger is bad, without anger major social reforms would not have been made.

- Anger which is destructive is anger against others or oneself.

- CBT can be effective in anger management.

- If you know you regularly get angry take some form of action to manage it.

- Assertiveness training is ideal in managing anger as it teaches how to create and maintain boundaries in a calm and confident manner.

BULLYING

- Being bullied can lead to depression.

- If you are being bullied, tell someone, whatever your age.

- If you are being bullied at work you may prefer to tell someone outside of work.

- Bullying isolates so it is important to find someone who will listen and is supportive.

- Bullying comes in many forms, physical and mental. Some will say that mental is worse because you cannot see the scars. Whatever form it can destroy lives.

- Do not personalise as this is about the bully, not you.

- People bully because they do not like themselves, not that they dislike you.

- A bully needs a victim who will not fight back.

- Jealousy is often the root cause of bullying.

- Being defensive can escalate bullying. Never defend or justify yourself to a bully.

- Classes on assertiveness can help in dealing with bullies.

- A bully needs a reaction, so remaining calm and being assertive is your weapon against a bully.

- Bullies are very unhappy sad people.

- Learn how to create and maintain your own boundaries.

- Your safety is paramount; if you feel in danger remove yourself from the situation as quickly as possible.

TAKE TIME OUT FROM WORRYING

Life can throw several 'curve balls' all at one time, or so it appears. Sometimes it is more than the body and mind can cope with.

- Do not try to battle it out alone; seek either professional support or the support of a friend or family member.

- Each day take some time out from your serious worries. We have discussed scheduling worry time but this is different; this is about life changes and traumas which overwhelm your whole life.

- Your body needs a rest from the stress and you will be stronger to cope, if you take time out.

- If you are enjoying yourself, try not to feel guilty; it will be doing you good.

- An art group is an excellent way of forgetting your troubles for an hour or two. It is difficult to think about anything else while you are painting and deciding where to put the next image.

- A trip to the cinema, theatre or concert.

- A week-end away.

- A shopping trip.

- Coffee with friends.

- Night school.

You may have more ideas but it is important to schedule this time into your busy life.

BEREAVEMENT

- Bereavement can lead to depression. It is part of the grieving process.

- The overwhelming feelings that come with bereavement can come in waves.

- These waves can often come when least expected and appear to knock you over.

- Everyone needs time to grieve and it is different for each person. There is no time limit.

- Allow yourself time to grieve. The Victorians set aside time for mourning. This probably ensured they managed the process more effectively. To try to recover too quickly can cause depression to occur at a later stage.

- Allow yourself time to cry. It is a healing process.

- The first time you experience bereavement it can be frightening.

- There are several stages, disbelief, denial, anger, regret, guilt.

- You can seek the help of a bereavement counsellor.

- You do not get over 'it', you get used to 'it.'

RETIREMENT

Retirement for most is a welcome release from formal employment and a chance to explore new horizons. The brain needs time to adjust to a new regime that is not driven by time and deadlines.

After the initial euphoria many can find it difficult to fill their time. There is no structure to their day and their life. There are only so many holidays you can take, art galleries and exhibitions to visit.

- For the first year of retirement you may not experience the 'highs' you had hoped for and you may experience a low mood.

- Many of the exercises in this book will help you cope with your new change in life.

- Some say, don't say 'yes' to anything life changing in the first year.

- Schedule your day so that it does not just happen.

- Explore new interests.

- Be sure to exercise regularly.

- Learn something new, a language, or a skill.

- Voluntary work. Something you really enjoy doing but be careful not to find yourself on the treadmill again.

- Bridge keeps the mind young because something new is learnt with every game. That is why so many bridge clubs have members in their eighties and nineties.

- Keep the brain active with word games, crosswords and number games. Keep dementia at bay.

- Keep away from the moan and groan society, they will only pull you down.

- Avoid conversations about health. It is inevitable as one gets older, health issues will arise but to have constant conversations about health and operations is to be avoided. Do not be afraid to change the subject, or in groups limit health talking time to the first ten minutes.

- If people have a need to talk about their health issues, suggest meeting up for coffee where you can talk health all you want without dragging down social activities.

- Build in plenty of time for fun.

LONELINESS

At whatever age, loneliness or being alone can lead to low mood and even depression.

- For many loneliness is just a feeling, but if you are really and truly alone without friends or family then seek professional help on how to overcome your loneliness.

- Often with loneliness you have to take the first step in meeting new people.

- Living alone can be difficult especially with the loss of a partner either through divorce or death.

- It can be lonely when you first leave home to work or go to university.

- The feelings are about the body and mind coping with the new change.

- Make the effort to meet new people.

- Join groups/clubs/associations.

- Start your own book club for example.

- Facebook and other media sites do not cure loneliness, they may help but real life contact is important.

- Coffee shops in churches are a good way of meeting new people.

- Be careful about internet dating. Keep safe.

- Many can feel lonely in a group of people.

- Aim to address your loneliness. Think of something new each day to make contact with people.

SUICIDE

This is a state of mind which will pass but it is hard to rationalise at the time.

If you feel suicidal or are starting to have thoughts of suicide it is important you override your thinking and take all or some of the following actions:

- For immediate help go to A & E at your local hospital.

- Ring the Samaritans.

- Contact your GP - tell the receptionist it is vitally urgent you see or speak to your GP.

- Tell a relation or friend.

- Ensure someone is with you until the feeling passes.

- When feelings of suicide pass people are grateful they didn't end their life.

- Children of parents who commit suicide never fully recover. Try to think what it will do to them.

- There is always something to live for.

- Life is precious and worth living.

Note for friends and relatives. Keep a close watch on anyone near to you who is very depressed. Check on them regularly.

RELAPSES

When the black dog decides to walk away there will be an enormous sense of relief and you never want to think about depression again and you hope it will never return.

Should you get a relapse it is better to be prepared for it.

- Put this book with all your notes in a safe place, in a storage box, together with your journal, highlighter pens and whatever else you used to manage your depression.

- A supply of mood forms from CBT.

- A new novel so it is ready for when you need it.

- Photographs that lift your mood.

- These are just some suggestions, you can add whatever you like.

- In classes, we named these boxes happiness boxes.

- Some of you may wish to continue with the exercises as they may be building your confidence.

- If you are prepared the next time low mood or depression strikes you will have the mechanisms in place to cope and that will make managing it that much easier.

THINK OUTSIDE OF YOURSELF

Many of you will want to skip this page but it is the most important page in the book. To think outside of yourself during the early stages of depression could be difficult, however, once recovery begins, just check on self-absorption because it is self-destructive.

Recovery from depression and low mood requires thinking outside yourself. People become self-obsessed which is understandable when depression attacks the thought processes but it is self-destructive.

If you read the blogs of people managing depression, look for how many times they use the word 'I'. They think they are helping by sharing their own experiences, when the best message could be to think outside of yourself.

- Notice how much you are generally talking about yourself, your feelings and emotions.

- Notice how many times you use the word 'I'.

- When we continually focus on our own security and happiness, we rarely find it.

- When we are obsessed with our own feelings and emotions we tend to shut others out of our lives.

- However down you feel aim to send a text or an email to someone asking how they are.

- Make the decision to take small steps to reach out to others however bad you feel.

- Note in your journal if the above two actions make you feel any better, if they do not, then you are not yet ready. Give it time.

- The happiest people are those who give out to others.

- The happiest people are those in the caring professions; they earn least but research has shown they are the happiest.

START LIVING

- Get out into the world as soon as you can and start living life to the full.

- Life is full of ups and downs; in time you will learn how to manage the down times.

- Have fun; try to see the humorous side of situations.

- Keep a happiness diary where you only write each day the good things that happen.

- Forget the past and move on.

- Learn to create and maintain boundaries.

- Learn to say 'no'. Saying 'no' earns respect.

- Make sure you build fun activities into your weekly schedule.

- Reach out to others, it is your own route to happiness.

- Laughter is the best medicine.

EASY WAYS TO LIFT YOUR MOOD

PART TWO

THE DENT IN YOUR WORLD

Dr Peter Connell

INTRODUCTION

It is to be regretted that the workings of the body are not a subject that is taught at school; for you have in your charge the most miraculous creation in the universe. It is hoped that reading this book will enlighten and enable you to master this miracle with which you are entrusted. Mankind so far has not excelled at managing his welfare in a responsible manner possibly not recognising that his genetic make-up has not advanced beyond the Palaeolithic Age (Hunter-gatherers of 40,000 years ago). Consequently, he does not cope successfully with the environment of modern living. This fact is constantly raised in considering the physiology, cause and treatment principles in this book.

THE AIMS OF THIS PART OF THE BOOK

1. To help you put in place, with concise and simple instructions, methods to enable you to cope with depressive illness and low mood whilst waiting for further specialist treatments such as 'talking therapies.'

2. To explain how these simple strategies are changing the way your brain thinks. How you are able to subtly alter the chemicals and pathways in your body and brain thus elevating your mood. This will also enable you to react in the early stages if depression recurs in the future thereby preventing it from becoming full-blown.

THE PRESENT SITUATION

1. Mental illness is losing its stigma and sufferers are more willing to be open about their illness and are seeking help.

2. Research into genetics, brain imaging, medication and 'talking therapies' is making inroads into the successful treatment of mental illness.

3. Discrimination against mental illness has led to the *Mental Health (Discrimination) Act of 2013.*

All this (with the accompanying cutbacks) has put added strain on the NHS, producing long waiting lists, resulting in the issuing of around 50 million prescriptions for anti-depressant tablets.

DEPRESSION:
A GUIDE

'We hold these truths to be self-evident, that all men are created equal; that they are endowed by their Creator with certain unalienable Rights, that among these are Life, Liberty and the pursuit of Happiness.' So wrote Thomas Jefferson in the American Declaration of Independence (1776). It is the purpose of this guide to help you in that pursuit for happiness.

Depression

No one definition of depression holds true, for there are many differing states of the mind given the name 'depression' ranging from Unhappiness, Sadness and Grief through to Depression and the Suicidal State. Depression is a disorder of mood. Normal moods are transient occasioned by circumstances or thoughts at the time. A mood becomes disordered when it persists, especially if it lasts longer than a fortnight. When moods or 'affects' (the two words are interchangeable) interfere with normal life they become disabling and are termed pathological (Greek - diseased).

Classification: Unipolar (a) Mild (b) Moderate (c) Severe

To be placed in one of the above categories depressive symptoms have to be suffered for most days over a two week period. A list of relevant symptoms follows later. (a) needs four symptoms of depression (b) needs six and (c) eight.

Bipolar (Also known as **manic depression**)

This is a serious condition and characterised by hypomanic (excessive thoughts and activities) or manic states of mind which often occur in a cyclical fashion. It may be that only one such state will occur over a lifetime and even then not be recognised. The symptoms of mania range from inappropriate elation involving non-stop talking, with weird imagery often involving extreme restlessness, grandiose ideas to the inspirational ideas coming out of the blue to composers, artists and writers. These manic states nearly always swing the other way into severe prolonged depressive states. The importance of being able to recognise this condition (even though no mania has been recorded) is that different treatment, that is lifesaving, is required.

Incidence

(a) Every year six percent of adults will have an episode of depression.

(b) Over a lifetime, 15 percent of the population will become seriously depressed.

(c) The incidence in younger people is rising; the average age for the onset of depression is now under 30 years of age. Six percent of adolescents suffer an episode of depression every year.

(d) Women are twice as vulnerable as men to suffer a depressive episode, even taking into account the man's reluctance to consult a doctor.

Genetic Inheritance

Women appear to have a greater level of anxiety than men. This may be related to their role as mothers. Their prefrontal cortex appears to have a greater controlling influence over their actions than in the male. Bipolar Depression appears to run in families. If one twin suffers the condition, studies have shown 70-100 percent of the other twins will also suffer. It is not thought that one single gene carries the liability for depression.

HOW CAN I RECOGNISE THE FIRST SIGNS?

Good question, as the doctor often has great difficulty in deciding (a) are the patient's symptoms the start of a depressive illness, and if so (b) how severe is it, (c) what kind of depression is it, and (d) what is the best treatment.

Symptoms of depression

The *Diagnostic and Statistical Manual of Mental Disorders* 4th edition (DSM-IV) published by the American Psychiatrists' Association, Washington is the reference work used worldwide for cataloguing mental illness. It lists eight important symptoms enabling a diagnosis of depression to be made, (see List A). To classify the severity of an episode of depression, and place it in the mild, moderate or severe category it requires 4, 6 or 8 of the listed symptoms to be present over a period of two weeks throughout which a depressed mood and lack of interest in pleasurable activities occurs. Often a patient will only present with physical signs, (see List B), not recognising his mental problems or not wanting to have depression detailed in his medical notes because of possible implications on insurance premiums.

LIST A

1. Feelings of hopelessness, worthlessness and guilt.

2. Persistently depressed and sad mood, a feeling of doom.

3. Decreased energy, a slowing down, fatigue.

4. Inability to concentrate, think, remember or make decisions.

5. Insomnia, early morning waking or sleeping to excess.

6. Diminished interest in hobbies, pleasurable activities, sex.

7. Loss of appetite with weight loss or increase in appetite with weight gain.

8. Restlessness, inability to settle or relax, irritability.

LIST B

1. Headaches; migraines.

2. Persistent indigestion, morning nausea or vomiting.

3. Chronic aches and pains including chest pains.

4. Bowel colic or bouts of diarrhoea.

5. Low back pain.

As about 70 percent of physical illness seen by a GP has a psychological background it is important not to take the patient's complaints too literally and to probe for an underlying psychological cause. Occasionally this is admitted as the patient leaves the room!

CLUES TO HIDDEN STRESS

1. Body Language: it's often helpful to go into the waiting room to call the patient in. Is he, or she, sitting relaxed or on the edge of the seat, hands resting or grasped nervously. Do they get up and smile at you or avoid looking you in the eye? Do they walk confidently or with hunched shoulders and head down? Arrange your desk so the patient sits at the side facing you where you can observe their whole body language. This can direct the whole tone of the consultation.

2. Life Events: The Stress Scale devised by Holmes and Rahe measures how likely stressful events occurring in the previous two years might precipitate illness. Forty-three stressful events are given a 'points' score according to their severity, ranging from 100 for death of a spouse to 12 for Christmas. The points are totalled: scoring over 300 and a high risk of illness is likely. Depression is commonly triggered by unpleasant events and bipolar depression is particularly vulnerable, becoming more so with each event.

3. A relative can accompany a patient so that the whole story might be told. Unfortunately mental illness still has a stigma attached.

Childhood and Adolescent Depression

A baby of six months separated from its mother can suffer from depression. Children can display multiple symptoms when depressed such as excitability, sleep problems etc.; but if correctly diagnosed and treated will suffer far fewer episodes of depression in adulthood. Normal adolescence is so traumatic anyhow with its hormonal swings and the inability to control impulsive behaviour, because the restraining influence of the brain's prefrontal lobes does not develop until the 20s, that depression is so difficult to diagnose. Couple this with college or work environment, forging new relationships, it is no wonder five percent or more are subject to depression.

Caution

Not all that weeps is depression. Remember to consider other causes. A poorly functioning thyroid gland, sleep apnoea from excessive snoring, excessive hair and infertility from polycystic disease of the ovary (the most common hormone disorder in women, with one fifth of all women possessing polycystic ovaries).

ACKNOWLEDGING I HAVE A PROBLEM

A Doctor's Overview

In medicine there are no 'norms'. Nobody is average. Normal blood test results always cover a range and often healthy people fall outside that range. Humanity does not conform and in that fact lies the beauty of mankind. One patient of mine (I knew him for years) would constantly joke and sing his words instead of speaking. When he was hospitalised with a sudden heart attack a psychiatrist was summoned and diagnosed hypomania. He was put on mood stabilising drugs. His relatives failed to recognise him!

Some of us are constantly bouncy, like Tigger in A.A. Milne's *Winnie the Pooh*, others are perpetually pessimistic like Eeyore. The brain sets its own baseline level of happiness which is different for each one of us and is probably genetically determined. If one wins the lottery and another is struck down with paralysis; one is in a state of ecstasy and the other in acute despair but they will both return to their original default state of happiness within a year by a mechanism known as *'adaptation'*.

The Patient's View

To acknowledge a problem, three conditions have to be fulfilled:

(a) Your mood must have altered for two weeks or longer. Bear in mind that you may have lived with depression so long you consider it to be the norm.

(b) Certain trends characteristic of mood change may have crept upon you. Here are a few: inability to make a decision; life seems to have no purpose, aimless; irritability; self-pity; sleeping difficulties; moodiness; no confidence; lost interest; no pleasure in hobbies; feelings of failure; lack of social contact; brooding on negative matters; disorganisation; procrastination; physical aches and pains, headaches; your friends are avoiding you.

(c) Dismiss any thought of being ashamed of suffering a mental disability as this could prevent you acknowledging that you have a problem.

You have to decide whether any event or circumstance has precipitated this illness and if so take steps to rectify affairs. Otherwise having admitted there is a problem you should seek help.

(i) Self-help: self-help books, self-help groups, internet information. (from a reputable site such as NHS).

(ii) GP, talking therapies, medication.

HOW DO I FEEL ABOUT MEDICATION?

How you can help your doctor

There are certain things you can do to help your doctor come to a correct diagnosis and prescribe appropriately. It is claimed that 80 percent of all depressions recover spontaneously within a year. Although commendable to attempt to battle through without help, it is not advisable. Why plough through weeks of hell when help is at hand? You should definitely seek medical help:

(a) To eliminate any physical cause for the illness.

(b) To obtain a proper diagnosis i.e. possible Bipolar Disorder or Anxiety State, and obtain the appropriate treatment.

Before the Consultation

1. Write down all your symptoms; this way you won't forget any and the doctor can consider and discuss them all.

2. Write down all the questions that you want to ask about your illness, then you won't come away having forgotten any concerns.

3. Try to produce a 'mood chart' detailing your mood (say on a scale 1-10), your appetite, energy and sleep patterns throughout the day and from day to day. This will enable the doctor to pick out abnormalities such as early waking or mood improvements towards evening or hypomanic tendencies and help him reach a diagnosis.

4. Document any recent significant life events and how you reacted.

5. Similarly, any family history of mental illness.

After the Consultation

If your doctor decides to prescribe drug therapy, you have the right to decline and discuss alternative treatment. This will be detailed later. If, on the other hand, you decide to try drug treatment, this is how you can add to its effectiveness:

1. After seeing the doctor, find a quiet place in the waiting room and write down all the important information acquired during the consultation.

2. Have patience; all antidepressant drugs take 3-6 weeks to have an effect and your doctor will encourage and support you through this difficult period.

3. Read carefully the instruction leaflet accompanying the drugs, particularly the side effects and interactions with other drugs.

4. So check with the pharmacist any over-the-counter medications you might buy such as cold cures and painkillers.

5. If your illness is interfering with concentration and memory get a 'dosset box' or pill organiser from your chemist to assist compliance in taking tablets regularly.

6. Ask your doctor for any booklets relevant to your illness.

7. Show every doctor you consult, a list of the drugs you are taking.

What Your Doctor Can Do For You

1. Continue to record a 'mood chart' to show to the doctor helping him pick up clues noting the beginnings of recovery or drug side effects.

2. His support is vital during the first 3-4 weeks before the drugs start to have effect. His encouragement can start the recovery process through the so-called 'placebo' effect (Latin for 'I shall please').

3. He can recommend self-help books and support groups.

4. The website Moodscope.com, whereby answering 20 questions, taking 3 minutes in all, you arrive at a score between 1 and 100 quantifying your mood level. You can nominate a friend or two as buddies to keep a watch on your score who will e-mail or phone when your mood is low.

5. The doctor will choose a drug with which he is familiar, has few side effects and is safe. He will monitor your response closely and help you cope with any side effects.

6. If the first drug fails to help you, he has four different classes of antidepressant drug to choose from: a Selective Serotonin Reuptake Inhibitor (SSRI), a Tricyclic, A Monoamine Oxidase Inhibitor (MAORI), and an Atypical Antidepressant (a collection of drugs working on different brain systems) so he might change to a different class or add in a further separate class of drug.

7. If Bipolar Disorder has been diagnosed, it is often usual to employ a mood stabilising drug such as Lithium.

If you choose alternative treatments for uni-polar depression the usefulness and efficacy of these will be assessed under 'Therapy and other forms of help'.

THERAPY AND OTHER FORMS OF HELP

It is a paradox that antidepressant drugs work by raising the levels of brain neurotransmitter chemical shortly after the tablets are swallowed but the patient has to wait 3-4 weeks to notice any improvement. The following is intended to help you attempt to shorten that waiting time for improvement.

Diet

People who eat a Mediterranean type diet (fruit vegetables, pulses, cereals, olive oil) are 30 percent less likely to suffer depression than those that eat a junk food diet (high in refined sugar, processed and high fat food). The brain needs a constant steady state supply of sugar so it is far better to eat 'slow release sugar' contained in foods such as muesli (sugar free), porridge or banana, rather than cakes, sugary cereals, jam or sweetened drinks which produce a rapid rise in blood sugar which is quickly followed by a precipitous low when brain metabolism becomes seriously impeded. This enables the neurotransmitter chemical serotonin, which lifts mood, to be manufactured optimally from tryptophan.

Tryptophan: found in milk, turkey, soya beans, cottage cheese, pumpkin seeds and almonds.

Phenylalamine: precursor of Dopamine (also lifts mood) from health food shops.

Avoid sugar substitutes (Aspartame) which can become addictive and worsen low mood.

Vitamin B group: These vitamins are essential for the synthesis of the neurochemical transmitter Dopamine: Vit. B12 (found in fish and dairy products).

Thiamine: Folic acid (beans, peas, lentils, broccoli, liver).

Magnesium and Zinc (from fish, green vegetables, nuts and seeds).

Other essential Ingredients in your diet for Mood Enhancement

Threonine: Essential Amino Acid found in sesame seeds.

Selenium: Brazil nuts are a rich source.

Omega 3 fish oils: these have a beneficial effect on cerebral circulation and brain cell wall flexibility. Studies have shown low levels of these in depressed patients and boosting these levels brought about a speedier remission.

Exercise

This is the last thing you feel like doing when depressed, but it has very positive results. You don't have to go out jogging, although a change of scenery may lift your mood. Exercise in the home can involve 'press ups', weight lifting, running on the spot. It can work off tension and anxiety, also it can release 'happiness chemicals' (endorphins) into your blood. Additionally it improves cerebral circulation thus increasing neurochemical production. Exercise is instrumental in the production of 'Brain Derived Neurotrophic Factor' (BDNF) which is deficient in depression and actually stimulates the growth of new brain cells (neurogenesis). This particularly occurs in those areas of the brain dealing with learning, memory and higher reasoning.

Sleep

Eighty percent of depression patients suffer sleeping difficulties. Spending hours lying awake brooding over problems can only lead to a worsening of mood. Below are tips to help you restore a normal sleep pattern.

1. Develop a routine in going to bed; do not 'turn in' too early, you just won't induce a longer night's sleep. No daytime naps are allowed.

2. No exercise and no big meal within three hours of bedtime. These increase your body metabolism.

3. Do not take any alcohol before sleep, this produces an abnormal sleep that does not refresh. Also visits to the toilet increase as alcohol is a diuretic.

4. No caffeine containing drinks in the evening. Bedtime warm milk is ok.

5. No disturbing TV or video programmes in the evening.

6. Your bedroom should be dark, warm and noise free (no TV) except perhaps a relaxing tape which switches off automatically. Light reading if this has been your habit in the past.

7. To stop brooding over problems: write them down during the day and write some solutions to them. If worrying about them prevents you relaxing, tell yourself you have some solutions and dismiss them from your mind. Then imagine yourself lying on a sunny beach lapping up the sunshine or a similar relaxing situation.

8. If all else fails, get up and do something to occupy your mind: read, listen to soothing music, or lie in a warm bath; or all three at once!

Summary: Most people need on average 7 hours of sleep.

Those patients complaining of lack of sleep, having been studied in sleep labs, have shown to be getting sufficient sleep. Those becoming obsessive about their sleep may experience such anxiety that they are preventing themselves from falling asleep. Sleep deprivation therapy in depression can actually cure 60 percent of patients in 48 hours! Unfortunately depressive symptoms recur as soon as 'normal' sleep is resumed. On these grounds it may be that depression results from an abnormality in the biological circadian rhythms of bodily hormones.

Sleep rids the brain of toxins that have built up during the day.

Sleep is of vital importance.

Sleeping Tablets: These are not recommended because they would have to be taken for longer than two weeks thus increasing the risk of Addiction (causing unpleasant side effects when stopped) or Habituation (with return of insomnia on stopping). They do not produce a normal sleep and cause drowsiness the next day.

COGNITIVE BEHAVIOUR THERAPY

Definition

The treatment of negative and self-harming thought processes affecting emotions and actions by talking and bringing about a change to a more positive and healthy way of thinking.

The Mindset in Depression

i.e. the habitual way of thinking. In depression all thoughts, events, plans, interpretations are viewed in a self-deprecating, defeatist, pessimistic way so as to bring about the disintegration of self. So the self has no worth, no ambition and no future. This constant train of thinking sets up in the brain a pathway akin to a learning process whereby all input is directed into pessimistic interpretations. This produces permanent demonstrable anatomical changes (the brain shrinks in size) and neurochemical changes (serotonin concentrations diminish) unless the brain is instructed to replace this memory pathway by an alternative. This is the basis of Cognitive Behaviour Therapy.

The Method

All events, situations and plans can be viewed or interpreted in two separate ways: positive or negative, for example:

'My boss has got it in for me. She is always criticising my work.' This could be looked at in an entirely different way. 'My boss takes a close interest in my work and is always suggesting ways of improving it and making it more efficient. I often ask her advice and we seem to work quite well together.' The process of CBT ensures the patient reaches this alternative way of thinking themselves and believes it.

Negative thoughts rule behaviour and lose you your self-confidence by persuading you that they are self-protective: that you might lose face or be ridiculed.

The CBT Therapist

Will ask you:

(a) Is there another way of looking at the problem?

(b) What is the worst thing that can happen (most mistakes or failures have some positive features or can be learnt from).

(c) Try not to always picture the worst scenario.

They will assist you:

(a) in highlighting your self-destructive models of thinking.

(b) by helping you discover positive ways of looking at a situation (as the example above).

(c) by showing you ways of looking for evidence for thinking negatively and guiding it to positive thinking. At all times you are assisted to taking control.

(d) in ways to stop constantly brooding and ruminating in a negative way.

The Results:

(a) Situations and relationships can be re-evaluated to focus on the positive aspects.

(b) By moving on from the past. CBT deals with the here and now. So you look at past events impassively, dismissing them from your mind and not brooding on them.

(c) By helping you to control impulsive behaviour and anger and remain quiet if necessary.

These new ways of thinking will replace the previous injurious pathways created in the brain, and having been learned will be adopted without having to think about them. Thus self-esteem and self-confidence will quickly follow with a significant permanent elevation in mood. Some authorities maintain that depression is due to the adoption and imprinting of a negative attitude by the brain in opening up old evolutionary pathways adopted by primitive man to foresee and avoid possible future catastrophic situations and thereby preserve life. A condition no longer relevant to modern living; see the Emotional Brain.

However, new research is showing that people who panic often deal with danger more efficiently than those who are calm and passive.

WHAT SHALL I DO WHILE I WAIT?

Your most important task is to hold on to the certain belief that the treatment will be successful. When you haven't the energy to begin a task keep this determination in the forefront of your mind. Here is what you must do while you wait for your medication to start working:

- Talk to your family and trusted friends about how you feel. They will then understand and be able to encourage and support you.

- Try to maintain any social contact that you may have had; continue any clubs you may have joined, pursue any hobbies. This will distract you from brooding and keep you from being isolated from life.

- Attempt to discipline your mind and thoughts. Any negative or self-destructive ideas must be immediately banished.

- Invite laughter: watch a TV comedy or a funny film; listen to radio humour.

- See if there is a support group in your area (ask your GP or ring the hospital to find out). The website of 'Depression and Bipolar Support' has addresses.

- Exercise every day: begin with simple callisthenics (press-ups, sit ups etc.), and progress to walking, cycling, jogging, swimming. Housework, vacuuming or cleaning the car for 40 minutes a day.

- This releases pleasure producing substances (endorphins) into the blood. These elevate your mood. Exercise promotes relaxation, sleep and bodily fitness.

- Diet: A depression busting diet is essential to reinforce the brain's framework so that the medication can work efficiently. A proper diet will help the transmission of messages into the brain cells and build up the necessary neurotransmitter chemical relaying information from cell to cell.

- Trytophan (essential building block) in milk, fish and bananas.

- Vitamin B12 (essential for healthy functioning of brain and nerves and memory and concentration) found in liver, meat, eggs and cheese.

- Vitamin B3 in fish, eggs, white meat and whole wheat.

- Magnesium in lemons, grapefruit, nuts, seeds and apples.

- Zinc in lamb chops, pork loin, eggs and wheat germ.

- Omega 3 the most important of all ingredients in dietary control of depression. Look for the Omega 3 constituents EPA and DHA in fish oil capsules, and aim to take at least 1000mg daily of the oil. (Check with your Dr first).

PLANNING YOUR DAY

Depressive illness is one of the worst states of mind known to mankind. This is because the mind, which is the essence of you, is ill. So your ability to reason about what is happening to you is greatly impaired. It is therefore so important to create a framework to your day that can be your life raft to cling on to and use as a foundation for returning to normality. Your day must involve: sleep, food, exercise, meditation, rest and relaxation.

Sleep

Contains two phases split up into various periods of the night. Slow Wave Sleep, occurring mainly during the first half of the night, is beneficial and refreshing (this tends to be deficient in depression). Rapid Eye Movement (REM) sleep, occurs during the latter half of the night. This is dream sleep and has the same brain waves as being wide awake, therefore is not restful and releases adrenaline and stress hormones and invites awakening in an exhausted and unrested state. Antidepressants suppress this stage of sleep. Awaking early skips some of this stage too. REM sleep helps to solve conflicts and unresolved fears but in the depressive state these may well be not solvable causing the brain to use much energy to no avail. See section on Meditation.

Eating

It is important not to suffer highs and lows in blood sugar levels throughout the day. Frequent snacks of a non-refined sugary nature, such as carbohydrates, are in order, to maintain a stable blood sugar. Vitamin supplements are an excellent idea. Although the brain weighs only two percent of body weight it consumes 20 percent of our daily calories. It functions best with about 25gms of glucose circulating in the blood stream; a banana's worth of sugar. Best to eat foods of a low

Glycaemic Index (those releasing their sugar into the blood at a slow constant rate). This includes, fruit, milk, yogurts, wholegrain brown bread, All Bran, porridge oats. If you add protein and unsaturated fats this will slow down the release of sugar from food, such as potatoes and rice, higher on the GI scale. Junk food is anathema to the brain (highly processed food with trans- and saturated fats has been shown to damage the brain if ingested on a regular basis).

The benefit of exercise has been covered extensively in this book. Make sure you schedule some form of exercise into your daily plan.

Meditation

It is possible that some depressions are purely a negative way of thinking, whereby the sufferer can only see any outcome of any problem in the worst scenario. This way of thinking becomes imprinted in the brain's circuits and steadily leads to a deterioration in the ability to function in a normal way. Added to this is the attempt of the brain to resolve the pessimistic thoughts and problems in bouts of REM sleep. This saps the individual through the release at night of stress hormones and lack of refreshing sleep. So perpetuating the disastrous situation. So it is important to take time to review your thought processes, and analyse them for negative and destructive thinking. The time of day when most people are on high alert is between 2-4p.m. (providing lunch was not too substantial). Consider the following topics:

(a) **Boost self-confidence:** stop thinking in terms that you can't do this or can't win or succeed. Repeat over and over again that you can do it and so imprint this in your brain as a new way of thinking.

(b) **Challenge all negative thoughts:** put new interpretations on negative ideas: your friend didn't ring you back, not because they don't like you, but perhaps the voicemail was not working, or they have gone away for a few days.

(c) **Visualisation Technique:** Imagine yourself in situations where you are in control and succeeding at tasks at work and getting praise from the boss. See yourself getting better and socialising more.

(d) List your virtues, blessings: family, friends, you've started treatment (these are suggestions).

Rest and Relaxation

Read a book, paint, find some laughter in a book, on TV, a film, phone a friend. Listen to relaxing music. Have a warm bath, sit in the sun. People watch. Solve a crossword. Gardening.

WHAT TO DO IF THE MEDICINE IS NOT WORKING

You the Patient:

1. Continue on the medication until you see the doctor.

2. Don't ask this question until you have taken the medicine for one month.

3. Continue on your vitamins and recommended diet, the exercise, the self-help group, relaxation, music and any talking therapy.

The Doctor:

1. Make sure that the patient is taking the medication in the correct dosage (if regularly forgetting arrange for the use of a dosset box to help).

2. Arrange for the patient to bring in any other medicines (whether prescribed or not) to make sure they do not clash.

3. Review the diagnosis: is there another cause for the symptoms (a) physical: an underactive thyroid or adrenal gland etc. (b) a side effect of another tablet. There are at least 15 categories of tablet that can cause depression, including the contraceptive pill. (c) are we dealing with a bipolar depression that has not manifested any hypomanic symptoms and does not respond to antidepressants but needs a mood stabilising drug such as Lithium?

4. Make sure the patient is continuing a sensible diet, is exercising, and having talking or cognitive therapy.

5. Patients with treatment resistant depression often exhibit high levels of immune response markers of increased inflammation and cytokines. Drugs that increase these markers such as are used to treat HIV increase the level of cytokines and produce depression in 40

percent of users, (depression-like symptoms occur in laboratory rats similarly treated). Treatment with anti-cytokine therapy resolves the depression. It could be useful to look for hidden infection; carious teeth or chronic inflammation such as arthritis or autoimmune effects and treat these.

The Family:

What is not understood is the utter loneliness of despair. To this the family (and friends) can bring companionship/intimacy by just adopting a quiet spirit of cheerful optimism and confidence, and that patience is needed for a complete recovery. Inspire hope. If there is no desire to talk, remain silent and demonstrate your love by being there and silently sharing their burden.

Do not try to talk somebody out of depression; there is no logic in depression and so no logic will rescue from depression. Encourage when appropriate. Practical help: shopping, cooking a light meal, cleaning or accompanying on a hospital visit. Try to watch a TV or film comedy.

It should be understood that reactions to depression vary widely from going under and giving in to a bitter struggle, to attempting to carry on normally. Depression may bring out hidden parts of a person's character; cruelty, anger or whinging and demanding behaviour. So be prepared!

CHRONIC ANXIETY
(GENERALISED ANXIETY DISORDER)

Definition

A persistent state of unease. A foreboding that something harmful will occur.

Causes

1. Ongoing threats to the person either physical or psychological i.e. to self-esteem, reputation etc. May be imagined or overestimated.

2. May stem from childhood abuse.

3. As a consequence of a traumatic event in adulthood.

Mechanism

Buried deeply in the substance of the brain is the original primitive (reptilian) brain. It is now covered with the coils of the modern thinking brain (the neocortex: Latin: entwining bark). The primitive brain is the root of our instinctive emotions; those that will keep you alive: hunger, thirst, fear. It controls the working of the body, heart rate, blood pressure, breathing and digestion. It initiates the flight or fight reaction through the emotion of fear generated in being in a life threatening situation. It is in constant touch also with the thinking brain (neocortex) except when it decides to go it alone in an emergency.

Panic Attacks

These are sudden disabling attacks of terror where the heart thumps rapidly, the stomach turns over, legs turn to jelly, fear takes hold and the wish to flee is overwhelming. Over-breathing (hyperventilation) alters the blood chemicals, (remember blowing on a dying barbecue fire, causing dizziness and faintness). This state is brought about by the primitive brain releasing adrenaline into the bloodstream, believing itself to be under threat of death. This has come about because present circumstances have evoked memories of previous painful experiences. For instance, travelling by tube, the train stops in a tunnel, the lights dim momentarily reminding the traveller of being locked in a cupboard by an adult as a child, bringing to mind the terror they had of the dark.

One in 20 people in this modern society suffer from panic attacks. Some are not as recognised as they are mild: such as feeling of unease and sweating, standing in a queue at the supermarket.

Treatment

1. Cognitive Behaviour Therapy involving an explanation of the mechanism behind the physical symptoms and replacing the damaging thought processes.

2. Medication: Beta Blockers prevent the onset of the physical symptoms and possibly the panicky thoughts. Antidepressant and Benzodiazepine tablets are best avoided.

3. Hyperventilation: Is treated by holding one's breath for approximately 10-15 seconds or breathing in and out of a paper bag, either of which will resolve most of the symptoms.

Post Traumatic Stress Disorder (P.T.S.D.)

Here the primitive brain is acting like a sentry at a gate. After a severe traumatic incident such as rape or a devastating car crash, the sufferer frequently relives the events through frequent memory 'flashbacks', dreams and nightmares. This gives rise to sleep problems, irritability, outbursts of anger, avoidance of activities and places that recall the event, lack of any enjoyment in life, dulling of the emotions and isolating oneself from family, friends and social activities.

Treatment

1. Cognitive Behaviour Therapy: coping techniques, anxiety and anger management. Relaxation techniques.

2. Medication: SSRIs.

3. Eye Movement Desensitisation and Reprocessing (EMDR): a treatment whereby the therapist asks the client to follow their finger with their eyes as it is moved across their field of vision whilst simultaneously recalling the traumatic event. It is quite effective and appears to work in far fewer sessions than traditional talking therapy. Unpleasant memories are stored in a different part of the brain from pleasant ones. EMDR replicates what happens in Rapid Eye Movement (REM) sleep when unresolved events and ideas are worked through and reprocessed and placed to rest in the appropriate brain section. Studies have shown this technique to be effective and long lasting. It appears that images from the eye are also relayed directly to the emotional areas and memory centres of the primitive brain. These centres deal with eye movements, spatial location and unpleasant images, so that a person whose visual cortex has been completely destroyed by a stroke or injury and is completely blind can negotiate a path around objects placed in his way and point to the position of fingers held in front of their eyes. They will react defensively to frightening and threatening faces (but not happy faces). This capacity is termed Blindsight. EMDR is beginning to be used in anxiety situations such as: phobias, obsessive compulsive disease, abnormal-grief reactions and others.

Chronic Hyperventilation Syndrome

In the acute version of this unpleasant condition, through anxiety, the patient will begin to feel faint and dizzy, have tight chest pains and experience tingling in the hands and face. They will probably believe this is a heart attack. An acute observer will notice that they are breathing much faster than normal. To terminate the attack it is necessary to persuade them to slow their breathing or hold their breath for 10 seconds or so and the symptoms resolve.

In the chronic version, breathing may only slightly be increased beyond the normal rate of 14-18 times per minute. This over several days could be enough to change the acidity of the blood and cause light-headedness, dizziness, unsteadiness, tingling in face and limbs, fatigue, blurred vision, insomnia, terror, sweating and palpitations. Diagnosis is by asking the patient to breathe faster and the symptoms immediately worsen. Treatment is with breathing exercises, relaxation techniques and to resolve the underlying anxiety.

Phobias, Obsessive Compulsive Disease and Hypochondria

are further examples of the nervous manifestations of an Anxiety Disorder.

STRESS AND PERSONALITY

Introduction

A doctor wishes to know, when presented with a stressed patient complaining of multiple symptoms, what type of personality that patient has. This is important as different personality types react differently to stress. If the doctor does not know, there is a quick way of finding out.

The Eye Movement Test

As noted before, each hemisphere controls the opposite side of the body, so movement of the eyes to the right indicates that the left hemisphere is in control. When asked a question, particularly one requiring a few seconds thought, most people's eye flick involuntarily in a direction away from their dominant hemisphere. This fleeting action at once gives a clue to their overall personality as dictated by their dominant brain hemisphere. The doctor can then guide the interview accordingly taking note of the different attitudes to stress in different personalities.

HOW DIFFERENT PERSONALITIES COPE WITH STRESS

Movements of the eyes to the right

indicates the **left** hemisphere is in charge, heralding an extrovert personality. These people tend to thrive on stress and the cut and thrust of competition. They are willing to try out new methods and success pushes them to higher levels. It appears that brain neurochemical receptors or certain neurochemicals themselves are deficient in extroverts who are constantly try to boost these pathways to get a 'high'. This stress effect is termed Positive Stress. These people tend to be near the top of the job hierarchy and successful at their sports.

Eye Movements to the Left

indicates the **right** hemisphere is dominant and we are dealing with an introverted personality. These people find it hard to deal with stress and they often react to long term stress by developing depression. They are much prone to psychosomatic symptoms (bodily symptoms caused by psychological stress) through bottling up their worries. By being cautious and not taking chances, but being conscientious and dependable they tend to end up in essential but mundane jobs thus keeping their stress levels low but not attaining top level jobs. Stress lowers their immunity to illness and they have higher non-attendance records due to stress induced conditions such as stomach ulcers, high blood pressure etc. Weight tends to increase due to high levels of cortisol in the blood and consequently diabetes is a likely consequence. This stress is termed Negative Stress. It should again be emphasised that neither brain hemisphere is completely in control but that personality is the outcome of a balance between the two sides.

Boredom or Underload Syndrome

Boredom can cause just as much upheaval as stress producing much the same symptoms. It occurs in the following groups:

- The unemployed.
- House wives/husbands.
- The retired.
- Those in uninteresting and repetitive jobs.

The solution

- Create a diversionary job: small time gardening, window cleaning, handyman, cleaning, home-baking for cafes.
- Evening classes, sport (badminton, crown bowls, exercise classes).

Summary

1. If possible confront the cause of the stress and resolve it.

2. Walk away: decide on a life change, admitting the job, the stress, the interest, the responsibility is not for you.

3. Cope as best you can: relaxation/visualisation techniques as examples.

PERSONALITY AND SUSCEPTIBILITY TO DEPRESSION

Personality

Definition: The unique combination of emotions and behaviour that identifies the individual.

Types

(a) Introvert: a person whose predominant thoughts and emotions are concerned about their own feelings and reactions.

(b) Extrovert: one whose thoughts and actions primarily concern the external world.

Consequences

Personality is shaped partly by genes or inheritance and partly by up-bringing and environment.

The 'Introvert' is:

- Nervous and anxious, touchy and sensitive.

- Passive, shy. Reluctant to meet others socially. Few friends.

- Low self-esteem. Gives up easily. Runs away. Relies on others to resolve problems. Blames himself for life's difficulties.

- Often obsessive and a perfectionist.

- Above all, tends to look at life in a negative and pessimistic way.

The 'Extrovert' is:

- Happy go lucky, doesn't take life too seriously.

- Socially very active. Likes meeting people. Plays sport.

- May have multiple girl/boyfriends and marry several times.

- High self-esteem. Not daunted by failure.

- Possibly not too conscientious.

- Is optimistic and adventurous. Is happier than the introvert.

The extrovert's behaviour pattern may lay him open to more accidents and hospitalisation (reckless driving, skiing, contact-sports), financial problems (gambling, reckless investments), family distress (divorce and child custody) and disease (alcoholism, STDs).

The Brain Anatomy underlying Personality

The brain is mainly divided into two halves and only connected by a bundle of nerve fibres crossing the midline. So we have a Left and a Right Hemisphere with different functions to perform. As a general rule the left brain controls the right side of the body and vice versa.

The individual's personality is governed by the relative dominance and balance between the two sides of the brain. With modern techniques it is possible to shut down completely one or other of the brain's two sides. So turning off the left hemisphere will allow the right side to take control. This right brain person's personality becomes sullen, despondent, pessimistic and unhappy generally with life. Emotions of guilt and anxiety prevail with a permanent submissive attitude. Conversely a left brainer becomes foolhardy, uninhibited, aggressive and abusive with a 'devil may care' attitude. Normally the two sides of the brain keep an eye on each other and modify behaviour. It is this balance that makes a person what he is.

Evidence from Brain Scans

Introvert brains show increased activity in the Right Frontal Lobe producing an inhibitory action on extravagant or life threatening behaviour. Any serious life event spreads widely in the right limbic system prompting prolonged brooding far beyond what was necessary to deal with the trouble, but originally would enable a satisfactory solution to be reached. Thus the Right Brain puts many systems into a state of readiness to combat a possible life threatening situation. On the other hand, a happy event will not endanger life and will be routed through the Left Brain, with far fewer consequences.

The Susceptible Right Brain

Those in which the right brain actions are prominent, and dominate the individual's thought and behaviour, (producing an introvert personality), are more likely to have periods of depression. Add to this some of the following factors known to be important in shaping personality and depression:

(a) The genes responsible for the inheritance of depression.

(b) Emotionally distant parents lacking in love towards their child.

(c) Abuse in childhood.

(d) Parental disharmony.

(e) The child receives no praise only condemnation.

(f) Parents making unreasonable demands upon the child.

Then depression in adulthood becomes even more likely.

How to Counteract the Trait of Depression

All is not lost if you live under the cloud of a family history of depression. The genes responsible alter the imprinting circuits so as to preserve life by making you imagine the very worst scenarios, and by engendering a state of pessimism, shakes you into considering all possible solutions. There are three steps that you can take to alter this imprinted gloomy way of thinking:

1. Block Negative Thinking: most negative thinking is self-destructive and lowers self-esteem. Stop to ask yourself the following questions: What is the worst that can happen? Is this problem enough to spend so much time worrying about? Write down all possible ways to solve the problem. Stop constantly brooding over it. Realise that some things are not as bad as they seem. Ask yourself if anyone else can help you with the problem.

2. Encourage positive thinking: eliminate negative words from your thoughts like 'can't', 'mustn't', 'never', 'impossible' and 'should'. Learn from mistakes. Learn from the attempts at doing things you thought you could not do. Positive approaches will build self-esteem. Cognitive Behaviour Therapy teaches you how to put these ideas into practice. Mindfulness techniques enable you to alter patterns of thinking and enlarges that part of the brain concerned with concentration, decision making and awareness and imprints new brain circuits associated with positive thinking. All this has been demonstrated with brain scanning techniques and EEG studies.

3. Distraction Techniques: lose yourself in hobbies and sports which give you maximum enjoyment. Sports with a regular rhythm give great satisfaction i.e. walking, jogging, swimming, rowing and cycling. Also, voluntary or charity work, helping the elderly with their gardens, National Trust, Wildlife Trust, charity shops are some examples.

Personality: the saviour of the human race

By having the left/right brain division it ensured the survival of early man. This had the immediate effect in early man's tribal communities of dividing the inhabitants into those who stayed within the settlement's boundaries devising plans to improve facilities (huts, walls etc.) and protecting the women, whilst those more adventurous would explore the surrounding area for food and hunt, possibly engaging a nearby tribe in warfare or negotiations.

CONTROL YOUR BRAIN:
DON'T LET IT CONTROL YOU

Plasticity

The human brain is perhaps the most spectacular creation in the universe. When you look at someone's face, it hides an organ containing 100 billion cells with an infinite number of connections between them. Reality is dawning that you can, at will, alter both its anatomy and initiate new pathways of communication between brain cells. This process can occur because of the plasticity of the brain, meaning constant use of the brain centre or centres will grow new cells (a process known as Neurogenesis) thus enlarging its structure and will also grow new connections between centres and cells.

Proof

London taxi drivers, having learnt the myriad routes through Greater London, show via brain scan investigations that the centre dealing with orientation and spatial awareness located in the hippocampus, has enlarged considerably compared to scans taken before they acquired The Knowledge. Tibetan monks versed in meditation on 'compassion' show such brainwave activity arising from the left prefrontal cortex (the source of positive emotion) that has never been recorded of such intensity, so much so that the centre controlling movement is fired up for immediate action. This ability is retained right throughout life. In a study of elderly nuns, those who exercised their brains most showed no signs of dementia, although brain scans showed the same anatomical changes associated with dementia as those nuns who clinically had been diagnosed with the condition. The explanation being that constant use builds new pathways around destructive lesions in the brain substance. In children this capacity is breath-taking: remove half the brain of a three year old child (say for a tumour or incapacitating epilepsy) and the child will grow up normally, as the brain builds new centres in the remaining half.

Imprinting

Any experience, memory or thought that is repeatedly recalled over time becomes committed to memory or imprinted. The process of repetition is called 'reinforcement' and fixes the pathway in the brain. This is how we learn poetry. This process produces new brain circuits and even new brain cells if necessary. By constant repetition this new pathway becomes well-trodden and becomes a permanent addition unless it eventually falls into disuse and becomes 'overgrown'.

If past experiences have included many setbacks, some bad luck, and lack of parental encouragement then your 'well-trodden pathway' will consist of thoughts ranging around failure: 'is it worth the bother?' accompanied by a downtrodden attitude. Now, if you were to embark upon a series of positive mental exercises every morning on rising, just as you might exercise your body then you would imprint (change the way your brain thinks) a new happier and more positive approach to life. I emphasise that you are permanently changing your brain anatomy so that optimistic thinking will become second nature to you and will not need constant training. You will have adopted a new outlook on life not only life enhancing to yourself but to those around you. This will ease your passage through life causing less stress and unhappiness, to others as well. This principle is how we can ride a bike, drive a car or speak a foreign language almost automatically. Again, this plasticity evolved to call up past experiences (memory) to escape life-threatening situations but we can use this facility to alter our approach to life's problems and climb further up the class hierarchy.

How to Apply this New-Found Skill

The default setting for the human brain is 'survival' and to do this Man has to be successful. So to achieve success in life, use your brain to accomplish the following:

Empty

your mind of all negative thought processes:

(a) by eliminating them from your mind. If an obstructing thought intrudes, banish it from consciousness immediately and

(b) replace it with a positive determination.

Fill

your mind with positive thoughts:

(c) firstly, you need to have a purpose in life, a goal to aim at and achieve. Don't aim too high, better to strive to jump smaller hurdles on the way, thus being encouraged by success at each one.

(d) develop the confidence that you will achieve the next hurdle and finally reach your desired destination. This requires you to build up your self-esteem by employing techniques (a) and (b) above, meaning no brooding on past failures and replacing those thoughts with plans on achieving your chosen goal. And constantly repeating them thereby 'reinforcing the imprint'.

(e) visualisation: instead of constantly brooding on past failures and anticipating further catastrophes and undermining any self-esteem you have left, do the opposite: look forward with confidence and brood only on past successes. Banish immediately any negative ideas entering your head. Visualisation is an intense imagination process. The principle is that you picture in your mind's eye, in exacting detail, every aspect of you succeeding in your tasks for that day and for the future. Every action that you will need to do must be practised again and again in your mind so that it becomes imprinted and automatic. In addition scenarios should be anticipated and plans put in place to deal with any hiccups that might occur, like someone heckling your speech. Imagine standing before your audience, looking straight at them confident in the knowledge that you will not be hesitant and have already tried out the projector and have the pictures in the correct order. Envisage the enthusiastic response from the audience.

Success comes through hard work.

(f) Responding to the Moment: Your method of response to a situation, criticism or a person may be critical to the progress towards your chosen goal. Never reply without due consideration as to what the consequences of your remarks might be. If necessary count to ten to stop anger or dismay getting out of control and producing comments you may well regret and place a barrier between you and your goal. Treat everybody with respect and dignity. Try to see the problem from their point of view. Could it be that you are in the wrong? Bite your lip, take it on the chin. Learn the habit of pausing and considering before replying; get this imprinted on your mind. Direct any criticism at the actions, not the person. This will win you more friends, induce greater cooperation and keep you in a relaxed state of mind.

(g) Obstacles holding you back: anger: often borne out of frustration through not moving any further towards the target or setbacks. Consider: is there another way to move forward, is the goal set too high? Are our set attitudes holding us back? Are we still holding on to our negative way of thinking? Are we unable to pluck up enough courage to take the next step? Here more visualisation may be needed with a touch of aggression. Self-confidence may need boosting and indecision tackled.

Take control of your brain before it controls you!

PURSUING THE WRONG GOAL: A CAUSE FOR DEPRESSION

Evolution and the Brain

The brain is programmed to achieve two aims:

(a) To enable the organism to survive long enough.

(b) To pass on its genes and ensure the survival of the species to the next generation.

So what is required: Primitive Man: adequate care and protection by the mother, aided by the hunter-gatherer father who also protects to ensure survival to the age of sexual maturity is reached. Concomitant features to this aim are an adequate dwelling and fitness enhancing food. Once sexual maturity is reached the next hurdle is to engage with the fittest mate. This entails being fit oneself, skilled in fighting and hunting (if male) and of high status (involving possessions) and leadership qualities. If female, attractive and adequate physique for childbearing, skills in weaving and preparing skins for bodily comfort; and child rearing. All this is programmed into the human brain almost as instinct to ensure the survival of the species by ensuring the most advantageous genes are passed on. This goal survives today in modern man and promoted or marketed as happiness.

Modern Man

In Modern society ambition drives men to devote their lives to acquire more and better possessions, larger houses, celebrity wives, high-powered jobs, all to achieve greater happiness! Their time is spent commuting to work. All this is driven, unbeknown, by primitive instinct but resolved now into the pursuit of so-called happiness. Those that cannot achieve console themselves in the adulation of celebrity.

It is said that we are no happier now than we were 50 years ago. If, as said, we have an inbuilt happiness standard, whereby whatever event befalls us: winning the lottery, purchasing a luxury car or losing a loved one, sustaining a serious permanent injury, we eventually return to our original level of happiness, then our happiness level is permanently fixed. So once we have obtained a suitable house, spouse, children and job, and are comfortable, it is pointless to pursue this transitory increase in happiness to the detriment of all else.

Although happiness may not have increased, the incidence of depression has. This may be due to a greater awareness as the stigma attached to mental illness declines. Perhaps it is as a result of the medicalisation of people's reaction to unobtainable goals. Is it an evolutionary response to overwhelming frustration, when the sufferer retreats to lick his wounds and devise a new strategy? Everywhere are advertisements picturing smiling 'happy' faces with their new purchase, be it car, TV or clothes, which will only raise their happiness level for a short period, leaving them to desire the next object. Evolution does not care whether man is happy or not, only that he reproduces.

The Solution

The answer is to shake off this obsession to desire more and more and to start to give. To divert one's attention, to get involved in pleasurable hobbies, sports, join local societies, learn to paint, cook, devote more time to the family. Altruistically become involved in charity work, local committees, parish councils, preservation societies. If your particular interest is not represented then start one. Get immersed, increase your circle of friends. Splitting your interests will act as a buffer against low esteem; a good performance in the local sports team will offset a poor performance at work. Favourable comments about your photos in a local exhibition will counterbalance a culinary disaster at home. One day, immersed in these interests, you may suddenly realise that you are sublimely happy. If you have to ask yourself if you are happy then you are not. If you don't ask, then you are.

The Happiest Man in the World

is purported to be a Buddhist monk, Mattieu Ricard who lives in a Himalayan hermitage and has devoted his life to the study of happiness. The basis of his happiness has been meditation and altruism. This sounds trite but when neuroscientists came to examine his brain with scanning equipment they found his cortex demonstrated a high level of gamma waves (which were associated with consciousness, attention, learning and memory) never seen before. Also, it was found that the left prefrontal cortex was greatly expanded, whilst the right was shrunken down. This finding was proof of his fund of positive orientation whilst his lack of negative attitude to life had caused part of his right brain to atrophy. Just like the hippocampus areas of London taxi drivers' brains enlarged, the more of London's streets they committed to memory. Fitting evidence that by repetition you can imprint new attitudes and ideas into the brain's memory circuits to such an extent that even its anatomy has to alter. A lesson that just as the body must be kept fit with exercise so must the brain.

Moral

'People attempt to live their lives backwards. They strive to have more things, more money, to do more of what they want. But you must first be who you really are, then do what you need to, in order to have what you want.' (Margaret Young, singer 1891-1969.)

DEPRESSION:
TALKING THERAPIES

Mind-Reading and Mirror Neurons

The Department of Health's Mental Health Strategy pledged to promote Talking Therapies for the treatment of mental health problems.

The Problem

There has been a spectacular increase in Bipolar II disorder (one episode of depression and one of hypomania only needed for diagnosis). Now one person in five depressed patients has unrecognised bipolar disorder. Back in 2010 saw 40 million prescriptions for antidepressants in England. These talking therapies can be cost effective in providing a cure.

Talking Therapies

These are methods whereby you may effect a cure by talking through mental problems and putting in place strategies to counteract depressive moods and dismiss destructive thoughts with a skilled therapist. They include:

- Cognitive Behaviour Therapy
- Counselling
- Group Therapy
- Psychotherapy

Why Talking Therapies Work

Talking therapies work best with mild to moderate depression.

1. Communication between humans developed to influence behaviour patterns in others. This enabled co-operation in the tribe and outside to build better shelter and to hunt efficiently.

2. Communication through the tool of language was able to implant new ideas, attitudes and actions into others' minds and vice versa. So individuals could be persuaded to alter their mood. From body attitude, facial expression and vocal tone it became possible to 'mind read' the emotions of others. Through MRI and PET scanning, it has been shown that three distinct areas of the brain have developed to detail this ability.

Mirror Neurons

Underlying this concept of 'mind reading' are mirror neurons; these are present in the premotor cortex (the brain area that decides what action you are going to undertake next). It works like this: as you watch someone perform a task, the very neurons in your own brain fire away as if to perform the identical task. But a 'neural gate' comes down to prevent the actual task being carried out. Similar neuronal copying occurs with smells and sounds.

If a painful episode is witnessed, such as a child falling down stairs, your own neurons will feel the pain and you may well wince. Those unfortunate to suffer from the rare condition of Mirror Pain Synaesthesia would experience the pain witnessed in the identical part of their own body and if a leg was involved could limp around for several days. These sufferers have to avoid violent television or film scenes otherwise they may suffer 'painful injuries' for days.

Sportsmen and women may have seen the perfect golf, cricket or penalty shot performed by an expert and have learnt the art of practising that shot over and over again in their mind. Studies have shown that this method improves one's game dramatically over those who have not practised and even over those who have. Somehow the neural gate has been lifted. Very young babies do not seem to have this 'neural gate'. If you hold a young baby (under two weeks old) close to your face and stick your tongue out in an exaggerated fashion, the baby will do the same back at you. Could the enthusiasm of football crowds be that each spectator is playing the ball in his mind in a perfect fashion and reacts with dismay as he sees the ball taken from him in a tackle?

The Therapist

So this mirroring effect has a great influence on the mind of the patient, albeit subconsciously, and it is important that the therapist is able to persuade, cajole and implant a positive and happy mood by facial expression, attitude, gesture and language. Could it be that any failure could be down to the therapist have an 'off day' and subconsciously conveying his low mood to the patient?

LOW ESTEEM:
A THROWBACK FROM EVOLUTION

The Original Purpose of Low Esteem

In any troupe of pack animals any preliminary skirmishes are quickly resolved without serious injury and a leader quickly emerges. To have a leader is essential for the pack to survive; he is able to dominate the females of the pack and pass on the superior quality of his genes and build up a conquering group. The contenders for leadership have quickly backed down and developed a submissive role, otherwise continual bickering would undermine the superiority of the pack.

Studies on monkey family groups and their leaders always show abundant serotonin in the leader's blood whereas the rest of the troupe have far lower levels. It was thought that this was genetically determined but if the leader is removed and a new leader emerges from the pack, that leader's serotonin rises to 'leadership level'. On removal, the first leader's serotonin blood level dropped to the level of the submissive's blood and when introduced back to the group he remained amongst the dominated members and his blood level remained low.

So do we not all have leadership/submissive qualities determined by our genes and influenced by our upbringing? Apparently not, studies on humans have shown that poor self-esteem may be the only manifestation of a depressive's feeling of worthlessness or guilt. Often these feelings can be reversed simply by the administration of an SSRI antidepressant, when even intensive psychotherapy has been employed. So raising the serotonin in the brain can change a person with feelings of inferiority into one with confidence and leadership potential; but so can determination and conviction, coupled with appropriate aids such as diet and exercise.

IMPULSE:
THE DANGER LURKING WITHIN

Serotonin and Lack of Self Control

Serotonin mediated systems in the brain tend to give a feeling of wellbeing and a satisfied relaxed mood. Whereas the noradrenaline/dopamine controlled networks produce states of anger and aggression, anxiety and foreboding (the amygdala). In addition many centres in the brain are the source of beneficial emotions (the insula) or are inhibitory (the prefrontal cortex). So one's overall mood at any one time depends on the interplay of these centres and the balance of the serotonin/dopamine nerve network.

Studies using brain scanning and post mortem analysis of the concentration of neurochemicals or their metabolites in the brain have uncovered evidence for the biological cause of criminal behaviour. Criminality appears when the complicated brain mechanism necessary for stability of mood breaks down. Certain brain centres become deficient in chemical neurotransmitters and inhibition of the primitive brain is lost. This results in violence and aggressive behaviour.

Suicide

This act is violence turned against oneself. Impulsive and violent suicides (cutting wrists, jumping from bridges etc.) have shown low serotonin levels in the brain, whereas contemplated, non-violent suicides (drug overdose) have not.

Arson

This is an act of violence against property, often on impulse and these perpetrators show low cerebral serotonin.

Alcoholism

People addicted to alcohol are in a worse situation. There is usually a strong family history of alcoholism, suggesting a genetic factor. In addition taking a drink boosts serotonin levels but abstaining sends the serotonin level below the previous baseline for several weeks. So the sufferer is sorely tempted to a restorative drink. Alcohol tends to depress the prefrontal cortex (the centre inhibiting aggression) more than the amygdala (the centre arousing anger and aggression). Couple this with the incomplete development of the prefrontal cortex in the teenager and you have the typical rowdy fighting crowd seen late on a Saturday night.

Gambling and drug addiction, vandalism, joyriding, shop-lifting

These all stem from a lower serotonin level producing a need to boost its level. This is accomplished by thrill seeking behaviour boosting serotonin levels. The risk taker who ignores the consequences. The thrill seeker who requires instant gratification with no financial gain. Anti-social behaviour. These acts will be repeated as gaining a 'high' from raised nerve chemicals becomes addictive. High testosterone in the young male also plays a significant role. Interestingly those able to afford it will gain their 'kicks' from rock climbing, surfing, sky diving, financial risk taking for example.

Treatment

(a) Diet. Serotonin needs a plentiful supply of the essential amino acid **Tryptophan** which has to form part of the daily diet. Normal diets only contain about 1.5G daily. It is required for other functions in the body which have to compete with the brain's needs. Sources of Tryptophan are eggs, cheese, fish, meat and poultry. Fructose and lactose intolerance lowers its absorption from the intestine. Supplements should aim to provide no more than 0.5-3gm of tryptophan daily. Vitamins B3 (300mg) and B6 (50mg) daily are helpful.

(b) Cognitive Behaviour Therapy should be able to teach coping and avoidance skills.

(c) SSRI antidepressant drugs such as Fluoxetine should raise serotonin levels.

DOES SEASONAL AFFECTIVE DISORDER (S.A.D.) HOLD THE CLUE TO ALL DEPRESSION?

Definition

Depression coinciding or caused by the darker days of winter and longer nights and tending to occur every year.

Incidence

Rises the higher the latitude. Alaska and Finland 10 percent with 25 percent reporting a lowering of mood. UK is two percent but true Icelanders have no sufferers. Female to male ratio is 4:1 approximately.

Circadian Rhythm

(Latin: circa=about; diem=day) Denoting the changes that occur in an organism in a cyclical fashion over 24 hours, enabling it to deal efficiently with activities necessary in the daylight and to wind down at night and enter restorative sleep phase.

Mechanism

This involves a centre of the brain (the suprachiasmatic nuclei) receiving direct input from special receptors (melopsin cells) in the retina of the eyes as to the light intensity in the environment. The brain centre then organises the release of different hormones over 24 hours to ensure brain and body are operating at maximum efficiency. A blind person whose retina is intact will continue to receive the signals conveyed from the melopsin cells. The study of these rhythms is termed **Chronobiology** and extends to include the female monthly menstrual cycle or the bear's annual hibernation.

The Human Circadian Rhythm

Examples would include 2a.m. deepest sleep; 4a.m lowest body temperature; 6a.m. rise in blood pressure to cope with day's imminent tasks; 7a.m. production of the sleep promoting hormone Melatonin ceases; 9a.m. Testosterone hormone surges into the blood for aggression and confidence. Then throughout the day measures are introduced to increase alertness and coordination, muscle strength and response time until 9p.m. when melatonin is released to encourage sleep.

S.A.D.

(SEASONAL AFFECTIVE DISORDER)

Symptoms

At the approach of winter, as days become shorter, the sufferer will tend to sleep on in the mornings, the appetite will increase, especially for carbohydrate-rich foods and weight gain occurs. The day is spent in an irritable mood, affecting concentration, lethargy with depressive symptoms of low esteem, guilt and worthlessness. Bouts of sleeping are common.

Causes

Uncertain. This may be a throwback to an evolutionary trend in the winter months to slow activity down, eat excessively to store up body fat over the cold months and virtually hibernate, living on fat reserves. The fault could lie in the melopsin cells (there is evidence for a genetic fault here) or the body clock centre ordering the release of too much melatonin, prompted by the lower light levels, producing continual lethargy and the desire to sleep. But it all points to the body clock being out of synchrony with the sleep/wake cycle. Body systems are not in harmony. Some unusual treatments emphasise this:

Treatment

1. Light Therapy: strong light (appropriate light boxes are available) used for 60 minutes daily, produces a remarkable improvement in around five days. (This must be done by a fully trained professional.)

2. Partial or complete sleep deprivation effects an immediate temporary cure. Naturally sufferers feel tired but they report heightened physical and mental energy.

3. Giving melatonin at critical times can reset all the effects of the body clock simultaneously and synchronise the two systems.

4. Antidepressant medication designed to raise serotonin from which melatonin is made, as well as coping with depressive symptoms.

5. Cognitive Behaviour Therapy to help cope.

Treatments 1, 2 and 3 point to an uncoupling between the outside environment and sleep/wake cycle or at least a misunderstanding between the two.

The above disorder bears a striking similarity to the next (PMT).

THE PREMENSTRUAL SYNDROME

Symptoms

characterised by mood changes occurring in the second half of the menstrual cycle: irritability, depression, outbursts of crying, anxiety, low self-esteem, sleep disturbances, appetite changes with cravings for sweet foods, thirst, water retention and weight gain.

Premenstrual Dysphoric (Greek = 'Hard to Bear') Syndrome

This refers to a condition that totally disrupts a patient's work and social interaction. It is serious and is now recognised as a distinct psychiatric condition. It is characterised by severe changes in mood, sometimes suicidal, and constant irritability and is more common in previous sufferers from depression.

Causes

Fluctuating levels of hormones: progesterone, oestrogen and the fluid controlling hormone, aldosterone. The brain contains many receptor cells for oestrogen and progesterone which are able to effect mood changes. A raised progesterone produces depression and retards the circadian cycle and a high level of oestrogen causes anxiety. Associated with premenstrual syndrome sufferers is a flattened melatonin hormone level rather than the fluctuating situation found in non-sufferers. Fluctuating or higher levels of melatonin are less likely to be altered by hormones, but at the lower level the hormones manage to disorganise the body's sleep/wake cycle and the release of the appropriate hormones at the correct times.

Treatment

- Hormones to suppress ovulation.

- Diuretics to relieve fluid retention.

- SSRI antidepressants to raise serotonin levels.

- Exercise raises serotonin and dopamine levels.

- Sleep deprivation therapy; restrict sleep to 4 hours on one night when experiencing symptoms.

- Light Therapy: this consists of shining a small blue pulsed light into each masked eye for 15 minutes every day for the second half of the menstrual cycle; this has relieved more patients than any other treatment. (Increasing carbohydrate intake also raises serotonin levels but inevitably leads to weight gain).

Conclusion

This condition is rapidly becoming recognised as a Disrupted Circadian Rhythm Syndrome because of the hallmark of sleep disturbance, depression and irritability due to inappropriate hormonal and neurotransmitter levels throughout the 24 hour cycle. It responds well to shifting the circadian cycle into harmony with day/night schedules.

COULD ALL DEPRESSION BE CAUSED BY A DISRUPTED CIRCADIAN RHYTHM?

Modern Living

Our ancestors went to bed with the setting sun and rose at dawn. Today we spend the daylight hours inside under artificial light rarely venturing out for any length of time. The elderly often sit all day in dimly lit rooms and their body clock thinks it is time for sleep and advances its time. We do our very best to disrupt our body clock. We stay up watching late night films, drinking coffee to keep us awake, adding late night snacks to confuse our systems further. Our parties persist into the small hours aided by alcohol needing to be detoxified overnight. We read by bright light to relax and then lie awake worrying and producing fight and flight hormones prolonging our waking hours. Life events produce even more chaos. So we end up with melatonin slowing us down with lethargy and struggling with tiredness in the daytime and serotonin, dopamine and cortisol doing their best to keep us awake at night. The body's only reaction to this extreme exhaustion is a total shutdown; in a word, depression.

So far treatment has consisted in trying to boost the low level of serotonin which may be low because the brain thinks it is night time. But this treatment takes 3-4 weeks to take effect even though brain levels are thought to respond in a few days. So we add cognitive behaviour therapy to teach coping therapy whilst we wait, and exercise to make us feel happier through endorphin release. We put in place stratagems to help recover our sleep and restore the regular rhythm of deep to REM sleep, this part could well be the most important part of the treatment. So why not try light therapy, known to work well in SAD and PMS by putting the circadian pattern in synchrony with the day/night cycle? The few studies so far in chronic stubborn depression have shown that it works well producing an excellent response in 7 days and even better if combined with SSRI antidepressants. Sleep deprivation works in one day, but relapses as soon as sleep is resumed (presumably at the wrong time!).

Administration of melatonin at the relevant times in the 24 hour cycle also realigns the body appropriately.

Could it be that we have always guided the depressed patient to the wrong specialist and should have sent them to a Physiologist?

SELF HARM AND SUICIDE

Suicide

Kills twice as many as die on the roads and is the most common form of death in young people. Doctors tend to avoid asking about suicidal thoughts for fear of uncovering a risk they would be unable to manage.

Classification

(a) Suicide associated with a depressive illness.

(b) Suicide not associated with depression.

The latter occurrence would suggest that suicide is a separate entity altogether occurring by itself or alongside depression but not part of the disease process. It can occur after the depression has lifted or even years later. It often comes as a complete surprise to the psychiatrist treating the patient. Many depressed patients may wish themselves dead but to commit the deed demands energy and courage which depressed patients do not have. It occurs in people who have everything to look forward to.

Factors Influencing Liability to Suicide: (not in order of importance)

(1) Genetic: a family history: confirmed with studies on identical twins.

(2) Difficult childhood, abuse: shown to lower permanently serotonin levels.

(3) Poor health: for many years, men aged 75+ had the highest rate.

(4) Addiction to alcohol, drugs and gambling: these lower brain serotonin levels.

(5) Low blood cholesterol: causes deficiencies in the insulating sheaths of neurons which break down and impair their conductivity.

(6) The low brain serotonin levels and excess serotonin receptors (to mop up all of the neurotransmitter chemical available). Confirmed by post mortem examination in suicide victims.

(7) Stress and negative life events.

(8) Previous attempt at self-harm: 30 percent of these will go on to complete.

(9) It is said certain antidepressants can lift a patient enough to enable them to find sufficient energy to go on to suicide. This may happen rarely. To combat this GPs should warn of adverse effects such as agitation, self-destructive thoughts etc. (ECT can counter suicidal tendencies effectively).

(10) Coming off treatment (even slow withdrawal) especially Lithium.

(11) Contagion.

Contagion or Copycat Suicide

Media publication or knowledge of a particular suicide may spark a local or nationwide spate of similar events. In South Wales, in 2007 a teenage schoolgirl's suicide by hanging was followed by eleven similar suicides in a year. A core of seven were linked by a social networking website. Incentives reported by friends of the victims were described as 'a trend developed', 'a fascination', 'a craze'. A kind of herd instinct was created perhaps by the lack of inhibitory control occurring in the teenage brain and their apparent immunity to the finality of death.

'Death was due to the Balance of the Mind being Disturbed'

This is a verdict that a coroner might bring in when the suicide victim was capable of making rational decisions regarding ending his own life. This 'balance' is responsible for a person's character throughout their lifetime, although this book is about the means to reshape it. This is a balance between the right and the left brain hemispheres which keep an eye on each other's activities. Freud summed it up as the battle between the Life Instinct and the Death Instinct. There is a rare syndrome whereby the sufferer is unable to exert any control over the movements of their left hand. Sometimes this left hand will attempt to strangle the sufferer and will have to be pulled away by the right hand which is under control. This is the Alien Hand Syndrome caused by a lesion in the corpus callosum (a sheet of nerve fibres connecting both sides of the brain enabling both to exert a controlling effect on the other). In this case a depressed right cerebral hemisphere (which controls the left side of the body) has been released from the modifying influence of the left hemisphere. This illustrates Freud's Death Instinct (Right Brain) gaining the upper hand when released from control by the Life Instinct (Left Brain). Freud explained suicide as a murderous impulse directed against someone else turned upon oneself.

Serotonin Levels

Levels of this neurotransmitter in suicide victims have been found to be particularly low in areas of the brain concerned with inhibitory responses. These low levels may be caused by chronic stress which also elevates levels of enzymes that destroy serotonin which are: genetic, poor upbringing, foetal damage from mothers' addictions to alcohol and drugs. So there is little or no curb on sudden impulses or aggression which are designed to retaliate against any threat or chronic stress. It is aggression without inhibition that produces violent behaviour or even murder and without inhibition this violence may more easily be turned upon the victim. It should be realised that in addition to serotonin there are countless other hormones and chemicals involved in regulation of brain function. Their nature and influence upon mood and attitude is beyond the scope of this book.

SELF HARM: SELF INJURY

Definition

Intention to damage body tissue without suicidal intent.

Method

(1) Damage to skin by cutting, burning, bruising or preventing wound healing.

(2) Ingestion of toxic substances.

Associated Clinical Conditions

(a) Borderline Personality Disorder, Depression, Abuse, PTSD, Eating Disorders and Schizophrenia.

(b) 'Normal'. As a coping mechanism under intense stress; with emotional abuse; poor self-esteem due to a history of physical, mental or sexual abuse. As a method of manipulation or punishment. Attention seeking.

Treatment

(1) Treat the underlying cause e.g. depression with antidepressants etc.

(2) Avoidance techniques: distraction, alternative non-harmful pain: cold shower, eat chilli peppers. Other pursuits: hard exercise, find someone to talk to.

Statistics

Unreliable as much goes unreported. Affects 15-24 age group primarily. More girls than boys. Three percent go on to suicide. Tends to persist as endorphins released with physical injury are pleasurable and ameliorate the emotional torment so takes on an addictive quality.

POST TRAUMATIC STRESS DISORDER
(P.T.S.D.)

Principle

PTSD is a psychological condition whereby past life-threatening or severely distressing events are recalled in vivid detail from memory causing disabling anxiety or panic. Recall is sparked off when only a small detail may remind the brain or suggest that the event may be happening again.

Evolutionary Background

The memory of the troubling event is stored in centres deep in the primitive brain (the Amygdala Nuclei, so called for their almond shape). The purpose of these centres is to warn the brain of impending danger by engendering fear and preparing the body for fight or flight. These memory circuits are particularly persistent and easily recalled. Any hint that the dangerous situation is about to recur (by a sound, sight, touch or smell) and the memory is vividly replayed, like a video in HD in the conscious mind, evoking fear and the need to react immediately. Simultaneously the body is primed with adrenaline hormone to resist or run. This then is a protective, early warning system to preserve life.

Risk factors

(a) Genetic: proved with identical twin studies.

(b) An abnormal protein confers liability especially if upbringing was subject to trauma and abuse.

(c) Hypersensitive or emotional personality.

Incidence

Female: 20 percent experiencing severe physical or mental trauma will suffer some degree of PTSD after one month.

Male: 10 percent experience PTSD after trauma.

Diagnosis

(a) Flashbacks or recurring bad dreams. (b) Persistent agitation, poor sleep, irritability, anxiety, anger. (c) Avoidance of factors or places which trigger the memory. (d) Significant interference with day to day living.

Treatment

(a) EMDR (Eye Movement Desensitisation and Reprocessing). This treatment developed by Francine Shapiro in 1987 is proving effective in resolving PTSD and is approved by NICE. It consists of the subject following with their eyes the hand movements of the practitioner from side to side across their visual field whilst calling into memory the precise details of the harrowing event. Often only three or four hourly sessions are needed to exact a cure. Controversy rages over the precise manner in which this procedure works. It appears that there exists in the human a primitive visual system whereby signals from the retina of the eye travel down to a small centre in the primitive brain, the Amygdala Nuclei, bypassing the normal visual centre in the cortex. These centres deal with life threats, fear and strong emotions and contain particularly vivid memories, especially of any traumatic episodes. As explained above they are rushed up into consciousness if any slight sound, smell, place reminds the centre of the original trauma as a warning to be 'on guard'. This action is not subject to the usual restraint of the prefrontal cortex. This centre can even recognise a threatening face and an angry fist when the visual cortex is destroyed (but the eyes are intact) so the subject is totally blind. The individual only experiences the sensation of the threat but he can turn and run. So while the subject has summoned the traumatic memory to replay in his mind's eye, the Amygdala has to cope with the waving hands and decide whether they are a threat. This scenario is repeated over several hour long sessions imprinting itself on the Amygdala by reinforcement and obliterating the traumatic memory.

This ability of being able to 'see' when the visual cortex has been destroyed is termed 'blindsight' and brain scans have shown that nerve impulses from the eyes end up at the Amygdala enabling a quicker response in an emergency than if impulses had to go via the cortex first and be subject to delaying conscious control.

(b) Trauma Focused Cognitive Behavioural Therapy: the other therapy of choice.

(c) Drug Treatment: aimed at symptom control: depression, agitation, anger and flashbacks.

MEALS THAT MESS WITH YOUR MIND

Introduction

Kathleen Desmaisons in her book *Potatoes Not Prozac*, 1998 has shown that simple sugars (such as sucrose) and alcohol may have the same effect on the brain as serotonin in people with a genetic abnormality of metabolism whereby serotonin levels are low and serotonin receptors are correspondingly present in greater numbers. Simple sugars will act in the same way as serotonin giving the individual a 'high'. The same process can occur with alcohol. This can lead to an alcohol or sugar addiction eventually leading to the need for a greater intake of these substances to obtain the same feelings of heightened mood.

Our Primitive Diet

Sweet foods, containing sugar, originally were not plentiful but were usually safe to eat and non-poisonous to our distant ancestors. To encourage their inclusion in a primitive diet they also induced a feeling of satisfaction mediated through the serotonin or endorphin cerebral reward mechanism. Bitter tasting foods on the other hand were often poisonous.

The Physiology of Taste

The way we taste is determined by the types and numbers of taste buds found on the surface of the tongue. There are five basic categories of taste responding to salt, sour, bitter, sweet and umami or savoury. The latter type was first included in 2002. The preceding types ensure that essential minerals were eaten; food that has 'gone off'; and poisonous food is avoided and that energy giving foods are eaten. Umami (a Japanese concept of combining flavours) includes foods containing glutamate and nucleotides found in 'essential' (meaning the body cannot manufacture them itself) amino acids required to make the body's protein.

Life's first encounter with umami food is with breast milk. Other examples are: onion with leg of veal, parmesan cheese with tomato sauce and mushroom, leek, cabbage and chicken soup (cock-a-leekie soup). Glutamate is found naturally in fish, meat and vegetables. Each amino acid has its own individual taste. Umami ingredients when combined augment the resulting taste far above that of the simple addition of each ingredient. Just such dishes would be gratefully appreciated by the elderly whose taste buds (which each contain a single hair) slowly die off as they age, apparently mimicking balding on the head.

Tasters and Non-Tasters

The number of taste buds varies from individual to individual (8,000-12,000). Those with the least number are deemed to be Non-Tasters and comprise 25 percent of the population. Medium Tasters 50 percent and Super Tasters 25 percent. This percentage varies across the world and is tested by using the chemical compound Propylthiouracil. This is a particularly bitter tasting compound with the non-tasters comparing it with water and super tasters almost retching when presented with it.

Serotonin and Sugar

Serotonin in the brain regulates your moods and maintains you on an even keel. Those with an altered sugar metabolism up to 1 in 5 of the population have a lower serotonin level in the brain. Consequently they are mildly depressed, lacking in self-esteem, irritable and impulsive. They crave anything sugary, for sugar can boost production of the serotonin that is lacking and bind more with the empty serotonin receptor cells. Because the sugar molecule has this effect on the serotonin product it results in a heightening of mood or even a distinct high. This has led to the term 'comfort eating' or 'chocoholic'. They are unable to resist starting a box of chocolates and have to consume the lot in one go.

Chocolate also contains Phenylethylamine, the pleasure chemical released during orgasm.

Unfortunately too much sugar intake will result in a reduction of the serotonin receptor cells necessitating even more sugar intake to produce the same 'high' a process known as 'Tolerance'. This ultimately results in obesity, type II diabetes, insulin resistance and a high cholesterol furring up arteries.

Beta-endorphins and Sugar

Abnormal sugar metabolism also causes a release of beta-endorphins: the body's own morphine like drug. Beta-endorphin is often present in lower concentrations so sugar can cause a morphia-like response of elation. These sufferers are often in a much lowered emotional state and are susceptible to becoming addicted to sweet foods, drugs and alcohol. Obese subjects are particularly vulnerable.

Treatment

1. Avoid simple sugars (fructose, glucose, dextrose, lactose, honey) as much as possible. Look for sugar content of canned food and drink. Artificial sugars such as Aspartame can have an addictive effect and should be avoided.

2. Change to carbohydrates of low Glycaemic Index (GI) that take much longer for the body to digest and are released slowly into the blood stream, requiring less of an insulin rush and less of a 'high' with its corresponding 'low'. Examples of these low GI carbohydrates are legumes, pulses, whole grains, nuts, fruits and vegetables.

    Medium GI potato, basmati or brown rice, yam and whole wheat products.

    High GI (to be avoided as much as possible) white bread, white rice, breakfast cereals.

A NEW CONCEPT: THE GUT: AN OUTPOST OF THE BRAIN

The Microbiome

The families of bacteria that we acquire in our gut at birth may stay with us for the rest of our life. Through evolution these bacteria have become of vital importance keeping us healthy and by keeping their host healthy, they thrive as well; a process known as 'symbiosis'. This community of organisms that inhabit our bodies is termed the 'microbiome'. These bacteria have developed the capacity (a) to protect and defend our gut wall from being breached by foreign invaders such as powerful and deadly pathogenic (disease producing) organisms; (b) to produce in large quantities hormones, neurotransmitters, vitamins and immune defensive substances.

Modern Diets

Consist of a high refined sugar content, copious gluten and very little fibre. This encourages the wrong kind of microbiome to flourish producing faults in the gut wall leading to intense degrees of inflammation in the body and the ability of inflammatory substances to breach the blood/brain barrier. Thus the brain then becomes the site of inflammation causing initially depression (inflammatory markers are almost always raised in depression). Eventually in more marked cases inflammation can cause the plaques characteristic of Alzheimer's disease (Interestingly, exercise also encourages the development of a healthy gut microbiome).

The role that gluten plays in all this is significant as we are all, to some degree, sensitive to it. Gluten's consistency prevents proper breakdown and digestion in the gut and this summons up the immune system leading to holes in the gut wall. The gliadin protein of gluten produces high levels of inflammatory chemicals which lead to a breakdown in the blood/brain barrier. The antibodies produced react with the brain tissue itself!

It also appears that gluten encourages the growth of a detrimental microbiome.

Microbiome: the second brain

The commonest of the good guys is the Lactobacillus and Bifidobacterium often inhabitants of probiotic yogurts. The good guys produce copious amounts of serotonin (90 percent of the brain's content). GABA the brain's calming neurotransmitter involved in memory. Vitamin B12 which controls inflammation and transmission of nerve impulses.

Born with a silver spoon in your mouth

Well not so. The poorer your country of birth the less refined sugar in your diet, the more cellulose you eat, the less antibiotics you take, the less likelihood you have of developing inflammatory brain diseases such as depression or Alzheimer's. Babies born by caesarean section tend to harbour bacteria from their mother's skin which is disadvantageous as they appear to suffer more episodes of infection and allergy. A trend is growing of 'Vaginal Seeding' whereby a gauze swab is used to transfer maternal vaginal fluid with its inherent microbiota onto babies born by caesarean section Antibiotics will reduce the intestinal flora as will chlorine in the tap water! Find out more in Dr David Perlmutter's book *Brain Maker* (2015).

Be kind to the inhabitants of your bowel and they will be kind to you. Keep them happy and you will be happy too.

We hope to some extent this book has taught you that you can manage your body and your brain and thus overcome low mood and depression.

BIBLIOGRAPHY

Blakelesslee T.R. (1980) The Right Brain. The Macmillan Press Ltd

Brockman, M. (Ed) (2009) What's Next: Dispatches on the Future of Science. Quercus

Claxton, G. (1997) Hare Brain, Tortoise Mind (Why Intelligence increases When You Think Less). Fourth Estate, London

Coleman, V. (Dr) (1987) Mind Power - How to Use Your Mind to Heal Your Body. Century Paperbacks

Eliot, Lise Ph.D (2000) What's Going On in There? (How the Brain & Mind develop in the First Five Years of Life). Allen Lane, The Pennington Press

Greenberger, D & Padesky C. (1995) Mind Over Mood. The Guilford Press

Griffey, Harriet (2015) I Want To Sleep. Hardie Grant Books

Hewitt, James (1982) Relaxation East & West (A Manual of Poise & Living). Rider & Company

Holford, Patrick (2003) Optimum Nutrition for the Mind. Judy Piatkus (Publishers) Ltd

Kramer, Peter D. (1994) Listening to Prozac. Fourth Estate London

Little, Peter (2003) Genetic Destinies. Oxford University Press

Martin, Paul (1997) The Sickening Mind. Harper Collins

Maltz, Maxwell MD (1960) Psycho-Cybernetics. Wiltshire Book Company, Hollywood, California

Mithen, Steven (1996) The Prehistory of the Mind. (The search for the origins of art, religion & science). Thames & Hudson

Desmaisons, Kathleen (2001) Potatoes Not Prozac (A Dietary Plan to Control Depression). Pocket Books Simon & Schuster

Morris, Desmond (1971) The Human Zoo. World Books, London

Nettle, Daniel (2005) Happiness (The Science Behind Your Smile) Oxford University Press

Nicholson, John (1978) Habits: Why You Do What You Do. Pan Books

Pease, Allan & Barbara (2006) Why Men Don't Listen and Women Can't Read Maps. Orion Books Ltd

Perlmutter, David (Dr) (2015) Brain Maker (The Power of Certain Microbers to Heal & Protect Your Brain For Life). Hodder & Stoughton

Ramachandran, V.S. & Blakesless S. (1988) Phantoms in the Brain (Human Nature and the Architecture of the Mind). Fourth Estate, London

Servan-Schreiber, David (Dr) (2005) Healing Without Freud or Prozac. (Natural Approaches to Curing Stress, Anxiety and Depression). Rodale International

Reanney, Darryl (1995) The Death of Forever. Souvenir Press

Solomon, Andrew (2001) The Noonday Demon (An Anatomy of Depression). Chatto and Windus, London.

Winston, Robert (2003) The Human Mind and How to Make the Most of It. Bantam Press

Wolpert, Lewis (1999) Malignant Sadness, The Anatomy of Depression. Faber and Faber